Contents

6 Time Frame Risk — 117

7 Supplier Risk — 137

8. Post-delivery Risk   159

Foreword

What is risk? Risk is the chance you take that things will not turn out as you expected. If you make a financial investment you take the risk that the gods, governments and markets will smile upon you and the value of the investment will increase to an appreciable degree. You take the chance that the value will not fall. You choose the investment according to the risk you are prepared to take - the greater the risk, the greater potential benefit you expect.

However, only a fool invests all his assets in a high risk venture. Only a fool fails to research the likelihood of his gamble paying off. Only a fool fails to keep an eye on his investment. Only a fool fails to act if the risk of failure begins to materialise. A prudent person will do the opposite. This 'management' of risk can be generalised by saying that in any venture risks should be identified, assessed for probability and impact and a decision made. If the risk is unconscionable then the only possible decision is to avoid the risk by not embarking upon the enterprise. If the risk is tenable then positive steps must be taken to control the risk, delegate it to or share it with others, limit its impact and insure against its consequences.

In business one of the greatest sources of risk lies in the contracts that we receive from our customers and in the contracts that we place with our suppliers. Without contracts we would have no business and it is through our contracts that we have the opportunity to make profit, reward shareholders and the taxman, and keep ourselves occupied with gainful employment. But the contract itself is the vehicle by which all of the very many risks inherent in this opportunity are allocated to one party or another. The objective of this book is to show how these risks can be identified, assessed and managed in practice.

The book is written from the perspective of a company selling goods to business customers. The word 'goods' is used generically to cover any product which can be the subject of a contract of sale. Although the advice given is applicable to any scale of operations, it is particularly pertinent to larger contracts where the risks are usually the greatest.

The material provides a combination of suggestions as to commercial risk management pre-contract, at the point of making the contract (eg clauses to use and clauses to avoid), during the period of contract performance and afterwards. In most areas of contract risk the customer and company are naturally in diametrically opposing positions. Thus it follows that the wary customer is not readily going to 'sign up' to all of the clauses, exclusions and other stratgems that this book propounds for the company. Hence, in some ways the most important aspects are those dealing with what to do when things go wrong, how the customer may be persuaded not to pursue his rights or how otherwise the company can avoid a liability which 'prima facie' may appear to be his. Provided the company remains within the law (and this book deals with the real, practical world rather than the clinicality of legal analysis), the commercial tactics employed by the company to best protect its interests are quite legitimate. There is no such thing as a perfect contract and both parties are entitled to make the best of the bargain they struck. If the rules of the game change as the battle proceeds, so be it. Nobody (at least nobody on the British side) accused Wellington of cheating when he lay his men down on the ground to minimise the casualties from cannon fire and yet the expectation of the French had been that the infantry would stand to attention, being shot at, until the cavalry were ready to charge.

The analogy with battle can be a poor one. A good contract is one where both sides stick to the bargain, things turn out as anticipated and customer and company go away having realised their expectations. In other words, no significant risks materialised. However, at the time of the contract negotiation, and certainly if serious risks do materialise, then the conflicting interests of the parties do come more into focus and can dominate the situation. With this picture in mind the analogy with battle is perhaps a fair one. Inferior numbers, lack of intelligence, late reinforcements and defective ammunition are amongst the risks of battle which require careful management. Their business equivalents – cost escalation, bad debts, defective products, late delivery and many others also require careful management. *Commercial Risk Management* aims to show how this can be done.

Principles of commercial risk management

1 Taking a risk

A gambler is someone who takes a risk. He makes a reasoned calculation of the risk of losing and weighs that against the possible reward of winning and the investment required. Everyone is a gambler and every business is a gamble. People assess the risk of bad weather before starting to paint the house or go on a picnic. Banks take a risk in deciding to whom they should lend money. Life Assurance companies take a risk in offering policy cover.

These are simple examples where the risk is obvious. It might rain, the mortgagee might default on his loan, the life assured might die prematurely. And yet in each case the risk taker does more than identify the risk. He also assesses its probability and its impact. Was the weather forecast good or bad? If it rains what will I lose (spoilt paint, annual leave etc)? Before we lend this money we must assess the credit-worthiness of the customer, if he defaults how much does the bank lose? Before we assure this person's life we must carry out a medical examination; if he dies prematurely what is the outlay compared with premiums received?

What is more, the risk taker not only assesses probability and impact, he also looks at mitigation and holds a fall-back plan in reserve. The house painter waits for the summer when the weather should be safer, decides on quick drying paint and, if it does rain, to put up his feet and watch TV cricket from Australia instead. The bank mitigates its risk by limiting the size of the loan and its fall-back plan is to repossess the property if the mortgagee defaults. The Life

Assurance company mitigates its risk by not assuring people over 55 and its fall-back plan is to avoid paying out by relying on an exclusion clause in the policy.

Thus it can be seen that taking a risk should mean:

a) Identifying sources of risk.
b) Assessing the probability of those risks arising.
c) Assessing their potential impact.
d) Adopting mitigation techniques.
e) Identifying a fall-back plan.

However, it is frequently the case that either this process is not completed or not done thoroughly. The house painter thinks about the weather but not about falling off the ladder or that half way through the job the EC might declare the type of paint chosen as illegal! If he does think of these things he may dismiss them as too remote or academic, which may indeed be the appropriate response provided the risks have been properly analysed. So risks come in three basic varieties:

a) Obvious or obscure.
b) High or low probability.
c) Large or small impact.

The bank can choose between not lending the money, lending it and relying on the mortgagee to repay, or lending it and requiring the mortgagee to pay for an upfront insurance policy in favour of the bank (not the mortgagee), essentially indemnifying it against non-payment. Thus, in risk management three alternatives present themselves:

a) Avoid the risk (eg do not lend the money).
b) Take the risk   (eg the mortgagee is credit-worthy).
c) Pass the risk   (eg to the insurance company).

The bank can on an individual case basis avoid the risk by not lending the money. It cannot do that universally because it is in business, in part, to lend money. Risk avoidance is therefore not an option that is always available. Frequently the choice is between taking the risk, passing it on or a combination of the two. This could be defined as the Risk Bearing or Sharing dilemma. In this context sharing the risk means passing on any proportion of the risk from 1-100 per cent. One hundred per cent is hardly sharing but in the real world the hundred per cent option is hypothetical as it is virtually impossible to completely eliminate a risk by passing it to someone else.

Commercial risk management

So far so good. What application does this have to businesses not obviously in the field of risk taking? Banks, assurance companies, insurance companies, venture capitalists, are all obviously in the risk business. Many other companies do not consider themselves in the business of risk. They see themselves as offering their customers:

- Value for money
- Quality
- Reputation
- Reliability and safety
- Engineering skills
- Design excellence
- Capacity
- After sales service

all of which could be summarised as quality product delivered on time at attractive prices. Indeed this is the meat of company 'glossies' and other advertising material. This is fair enough, particularly when aimed at consumers. However, this book is not about consumer sales, nor is it about selling techniques. It is about risk in commercial transactions. In commercial transactions risk is being bought and sold and it is this principle which is at the very heart of the book.

To put this into some sort of framework, consider the objectives of the company (Figure 1.1).

figure 1.1 Hierarchy of Objectives

Corporate Mission Statement → To be the best company in the world

Local Mission Statement → To be the best division in the company

Commercial Objectives → ?

Individuals' Objectives → To fix the software this week

This illustrates that a link must be found between top level 'mission statements' which, while of great importance in overall goal setting terms, tend to be a little nebulous and the concrete, specific tasks which individuals carry out. The linkage can be found in a set of commercial objectives (Figure 1.2) which are common to all profit making concerns.

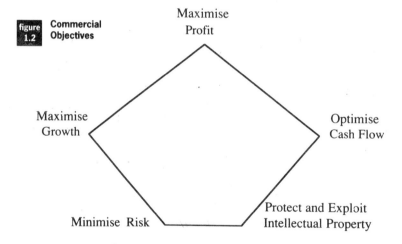

figure 1.2 Commercial Objectives

Maximise Profit

Maximise Growth

Optimise Cash Flow

Minimise Risk

Protect and Exploit Intellectual Property

If all company employees, whether at the top or bottom of the organisation, concentrate on maximising profit, maximising growth, optimising cash flow, protecting intellectual property (the single most valuable asset of most companies) and minimising risk, then all will be well.

This book concentrates on the risk element of the equation. It is appropriate to refer to an equation. because often the five commercial objectives are linked, appear to be in conflict or mutually exclusive in terms of the objectives of a contract negotiation. For example, lower prices achieved by reducing profit might improve growth but at the expense of the 'bottom line'. Accepting contracts without a proper review of the terms might accelerate order intake but will increase risk to the business. Excessive protectionism over intellectual property rights might prejudice orders from those customers who have a legitimate need to gain certain licences or other rights from the company. Thus the five elements must be kept sensibly in balance.

So a priority is the minimisation of risk. If a typical project is imagined of not insignificant value, to be executed over perhaps months or years and involving a lot of people and a mass of technology, then traditionally risk is considered from the purely technical viewpoint (will the software work?), and from the purely programme perspective (can we build it inside three years?).

Traditionally risk analysis techniques are used to identify these technical and programme risks which are then managed using sound project management procedures. This book aims to show that these risks have a contractual dimension as well as a project management dimension. It will also be shown that there are other inherent risks (eg supplier risks and third party risks) which are quite separate from the technical and programme risks.

So Commercial Risk Management can be defined as the management from a contractual viewpoint of all the risks inherent in carrying out a project.

Of course it is important to be sure that whatever the intended commercial transaction, it is legal in the first place. The law will not enforce illegal contracts, but since it must be assumed that readers of this book are unlikely to be dealers in unlawful drugs or procurers of criminal acts, the question must be asked as to where lies the risk of illegality in 'normal' business transactions. There is a considerable body of legalisation with which businesses have to comply ranging from employment law to VAT regulations. However, matters such as these affect the running of the business and usually have no immediate impact on particular contracts. The risk area regarding specific contracts or markets is in competition law. As an essential part of good commercial risk management it is important that contractual agreements such as sales orders, purchase orders, consortium agreements and the like contain only those restrictive provisions which are permissible within the UK and EC law and regulations.

3. The risk pendulum

In any commercial transaction it is inevitable that all the implicit risks will be borne by one party or the other. It may take a court of law after the event to determine on which side of the barrier an implied risk lay but surely enough all the risks lie somewhere. Perhaps in an ideal world the risk pendulum would lie perfectly balanced between the two sides (Figure 1.3).

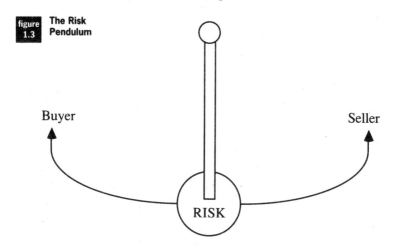

figure 1.3 The Risk Pendulum

Buyer

Seller

RISK

However, in reality the position of the pendulum largely depends upon the bargaining position of the two sides. Theoretically it should be decided purely on the basis of which side can best cope with or absorb the risk. For example, in a contract in which a UK company is buying from a US supplier the question will arise as to whether payment of the contract price should be in Sterling or Dollars. Another way of looking at this is to say that either buyer or seller must take the risk of adverse movement in the Sterling/Dollar exchange rate. Each will prefer its own national currency. If the US company also makes purchases from the UK in Sterling he is in the best position to avoid the currency risk by using Sterling earned in one transaction to fund another transaction. He is logically in the better position. On the other hand, if the US company wishes to be paid in Dollars, it will get its way if the UK company has no alternative source of the product.

This swing of the pendulum on the basis of bargaining power is well illustrated by the change in defence procurement policies brought about by the UK Government between the 1970s and the 1990s. In the earlier period defence procurement was characterised by:

a) Cost-plus contracts.
b) Procurement decisions based on paper studies.
c) Little competition.
d) Serious delays.
e) Under-performance against specification.
f) No recourse or remedy against contractors.

The nature of the procurement policy and the type of contracts placed left all risk with the Government. Cost-plus contracts, whereby contract prices were agreed at the end of the contract based on reimbursement of actual costs incurred plus a fixed percentage rate of profit, provided no incentive for companies to contain costs. All expenditure beyond the estimated costs fell to the Government's account. The then project life cycle (feasibility, project definition, development, production, support) frequently had major commitment to development decided upon no more than paper reports emerging from project definition. Thus the technical risk inherent in development lay with the Government for having decided to proceed to that phase. For major systems and weapons there was little competition as the Government awarded contracts to the major UK defence companies on, it was said, a 'buggins turn' basis. This effectively tied the Government to the chosen company no matter how good or bad its performance. In being so tied the Government had little choice but to accept late delivery and little choice but to accept under-performance against the specification. If the equipment under-performed, was late in delivery and exhibited poor reliability in service, then the Government had virtually no remedy against the company because the development contracts under the cost-plus arrangements were 'non-risk' to the company and, in any event, it was policy to support in-service equipment by placing further contracts with the original designer/manufacturer.

Under that regime all financial, commercial, technical, performance and delivery risk lay with the Government. The new policies turned this on its head under an over-arching philosophy of putting risk with the company. Many techniques were adopted and against the previous characteristics the following devices were deployed:

Old	New
Cost-plus prices	Firm prices
Decisions based on paper	Decisions based on technology demonstration
Little competition	Only competition
Serious delays	Penalties for delay
Under performance	Rolling liabilities
No remedies	Contractual and legal rights

In a short space of time the risk pendulum swung from its extreme position with the Government to an equally extreme position with the industry. Many companies were badly damaged, particularly in those projects involving a high degree of software development, by finding that firm price, high risk contracts bid in competition against exacting specifications and tight time frames were impossible to complete on time and within budget.

Here lies a golden rule of successful commercial risk management. As the Government found, it is sound policy in principle to ensure that contractual and legal risk lies with the other side. It is good practice to construct contracts so as to maximise the commercial incentive on the other side to do well. However, these approaches do not necessarily in themselves eliminate risk to project success. It is comforting to know that when disaster has descended someone else is liable for the consequences, but it does not actually prevent the consequences from being suffered.

In any complex contract it is as well for both parties to work together for mutual success even within the confines of a proper contractual relationship. It is unwise to feel contented merely by having achieved a massive swing of the pendulum. The 'tautest' contract can fix liability, it cannot guarantee quality and timely performance.

Nevertheless, the experience in the defence industry shows that the pendulum can be made to swing more by bargaining power than by logic. Logically the Government was better able to survive large project cost increases than companies with much more limited assets but the vastly superior bargaining power of the Government meant that the risk was transferred.

Risk bearing, risk sharing

Conventionally, a contract is defined as

'A legally binding exchange of promises.'

For example, the seller promises to deliver the goods and pass title. The buyer promises to pay the agreed price.

Non-conventionally, a contract could be defined as

'The vehicle by which the risks inherent in the transaction are allocated as between buyer and seller.'

For example, the seller agrees to carry the risk of loss or damage to the goods until delivery. The buyer agrees to carry the risk that the goods will or will not meet his purpose.

It is sometimes said that the contract serves no practical purpose. If everything goes well the contract stays in the filing cabinet gathering dust. If things go wrong the contract is of no use since it does not legislate for the particular problem that has arisen. This is short-sighted in so far as most contracts probably lie somewhere between those two extremes and, in any event, if the non-conventional definition proposed above is accepted, then it is to the contract that the parties must turn as a starting point in establishing ownership of and liability for the risk which has given rise to the problem.

So, in the sense that the contract provides the vehicle for allocating risk, what then in simple terms is this risk? The risk is that the contract did not turn out as the parties intended (Figure 1.4).

figure 1.4	Contract Failure

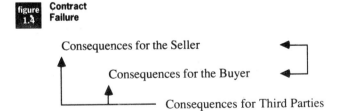

If things do not work out the buyer and seller may have liabilities to each other. Either or both may have liabilities to affected third parties. Again, in simple terms the parties' expectations were quite straightforward (Figure 1.5).

| figure 1.5 | The Parties' Expectations |

Seller Expected	Buyer Expected	The 'World Expected'
■ To get paid	■ Performance on time	
■ To transfer title and risk	■ Performance to spec	
■ The Buyer to take delivery and accept the goods	■ Performance to quality	Not to be interfered with
■ To complete the job within budget	■ To acquire title	
■ To be left alone	■ To be left alone	

The one common expectation between buyer, seller and the rest of the world is that each should be left alone or not interfered with as a result of the transaction between buyer and seller. The buyer expected to receive the goods and be happy with them. The seller expected to be paid by a contented customer. This private arrangement was not expected to come to the notice of the world. However, the car manufacturer who buys defective brake components and innocently sells them on to a motorist whose new car crashes, causing injury, will find himself in all sorts of problems.

Nevertheless, it is the contract between buyer and seller that provides the principal medium for establishing where the liability lies. In the example just given the car manufacturer and injured third parties may have action in negligence against the brake component supplier but, as between manufacturer and supplier, the strongest claim against the supplier could be based upon breach of contract (eg breach of express terms, such as the goods not meeting their specification or of a warranty that they are free of hazard and defect), or upon breach of implied undertakings as to satisfactory quality or fitness for purpose. This *could* be the strongest case depending inevitably on the specific contract terms and in particular on the effect on any so-called exclusion clauses, a point which will be covered later in this chapter.

The contract allocates risk between the parties. But before drafting and negotiating the contract the parties need to be clear on the nature of the relationship which they seek to establish between them. The relationship should be considered on the basis of risk, value and duration (Figure 1.6).

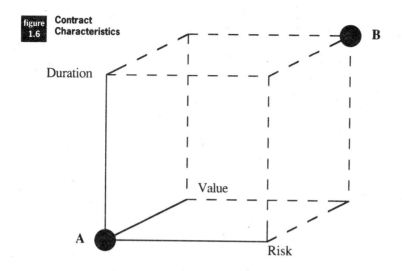

figure 1.6 Contract Characteristics

Where the transaction is in a zone close to point A in Figure 1.6, then a simple 'arm's length' relationship is appropriate. As the type of transaction moves towards point B, then some form of partnership is usually more suited to the circumstances. Where there is low risk in a short duration, low value transaction, simple contracts are acceptable. Any combination of high risk, high value or long duration demands more considered thought.

When a company decides to procure rather than undertake all the project activities itself it must consider three essential elements:

Procurement Type:	Non-competitive (sole source)
	Non-competitive (non-monopoly)
	Partnership sourcing
	Competitive arm's-length
Pricing Regime :	Cost reimbursement
	Cost incentive
	Fixed price
	Firm price
Contract Strategy :	Service only
	Design only
	Make only
	Turnkey

Chapter 7 explores these principles in detail from the buyer's perspective, but for now the aim is to examine this question of the nature of the commercial relationship at a more fundamental level.

Earlier in this chapter the golden rule of commercial risk management was discussed. This might be summarised as:

'There is more to minimising project risk than ensuring that the contractual risk pendulum has swung away from you.'

While in large part the theme and motive of this book is to show how to swing the contractual risk pendulum away, it would be an incomplete picture if the analysis were left there. In the cut and thrust of contract negotiations buyer and seller are both trying to push the pendulum towards the other, and it can be a demanding intellectual leap for them to consider alternative arrangements based on sharing rather than bearing risk.

5 Partnership sourcing and partnership contracting

There are two main varieties of arrangement between buyer and seller that can be used depending upon the nature of the activity. Both are based on the principle of partnership. Both assume that partnership reduces project risk while not interfering with the allocation of contractual risk, albeit that 'in the spirit of partnership', contractual remedies may consciously be set aside in the event of a problem so as best to preserve the broader benefits of that partnership. The two varieties are partnership sourcing and partnership contracting. These partnerships are not partnerships in the strict legal sense, rather they are concepts for promoting cooperation and openness.

Partnership sourcing is convenient when buyer and seller are quite remote. A car factory may adopt partnership sourcing to achieve a number of aims. The benefits may include a smaller number of suppliers, reduced overhead burden, improved quality, timelier delivery, commitment to problem solving and responsiveness to evolving needs. However, the automotive component supplier and Joe Public buying his new car through a dealer are remote in the sense that they do not expect to come into frequent contact with each other. In comparison with the end product, a car (a single high value item), the supplier provides dozens, hundreds or thousands of relatively low value items. The car buyer does not see the summation of thousands of components, he sees only the one end product. A power generating company may go for partnership sourcing for essential components to achieve lower price, very high reliability and after sales services. The end product, amperes down the wires, bears no resemblance to the generating components and the user, whether industrial or consumer, sees only that his air conditioning plant or television works.

Partnership sourcing is also at its best when there are potentially many suppliers from whom a smaller number of 'partners' can be selected.

Partnership contracting on the other hand has the supplier and buyer working much more closely in concept towards meeting the end customer's needs. This is more appropriate where a single customer has a large unique order for a single special requirement, particularly where a high level of research, design or development is required. A new weapons system, a new satellite ground station, a new aircraft, all can benefit from partnership contracting as the intimacy between buyer and seller so necessary on projects of this nature can evolve into a more effective commercial entity.

In moving away from arm's-length contracting the choice between partnership sourcing and partnership contracting can be characterised as follows:

Partnership Sourcing	**Partnership Contracting**
■ Many potential suppliers	■ Possibly sole source suppliers
■ Many end customers	■ Single end customer
■ Many supplier products	■ Single/few products
■ Off the shelf products	■ High development content

In both varieties a single supplier may provide a product which is critical to the successful performance by the buyer of his contract with the end customer. However, in partnership sourcing the supplier product, although critical, is either not used at all in the end result (eg pumps for power generation) or is only a minor component (eg the brake pads in a car). In partnership contracting the supplier contribution is a major element of the end result (eg the undercarriage and control system in an aircraft). Indeed in some examples of partnership contracting the supplier element may be of higher value than the buyer content (Figure 1.7).

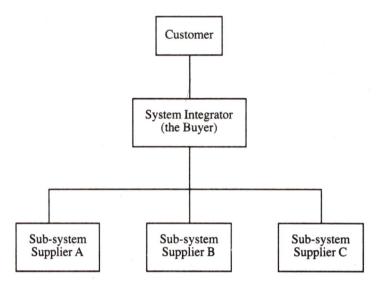

In this scenario the monetary value of the system integrator's work may be quite low in comparison with the work of the sub-system suppliers and yet, as between himself and the end customer, he takes the entire risk in the performance of the system. In this situation the advantages of sharing that risk with the major suppliers is obvious.

6. Approaches to partnership contracting

The principle of partnership contracting in comparison with alternative commercial relationships can be seen in Figure 1.8.

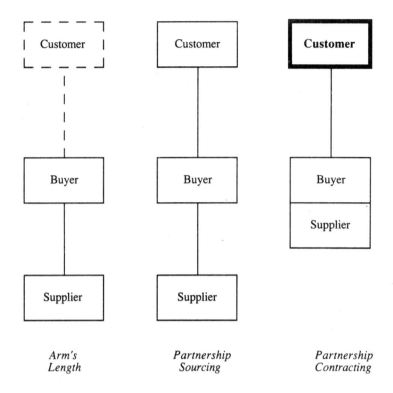

figure 1.8 Commercial Relationships Compared

The progression can be seen as the level of importance of satisfying the end customer. In an arm's length relationship the supplier is little concerned with the end customer. His vision is narrow and limited to completing his order. In partnership sourcing the supplier has a wider vision and understands that his endeavours will help the buyer to perform well, but his main focus is still in satisfying the terms of his order from the buyer. In partnership contracting the end customer looms larger and the supplier focus has shifted towards contributing to the performance of the end customer order.

There are three ways for the parties to organise themselves in order to achieve a partnership contracting arrangement (Figure 1.9).

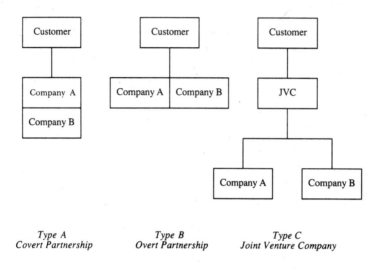

figure 1.9 Commercial Relationships Compared

Type A *Covert Partnership*	*Type B* *Overt Partnership*	*Type C* *Joint Venture Company*

In a covert partnership the parties would conduct themselves as follows:

a) A would negotiate with the customer.

b) A would provide B with sight of all or part of the draft contracts and invite comments.

c) The contract between A and B may require B to participate in the performance of the contract between A and the customer or of a particular part only (eg a specification).

d) The contract between the customer and A would be accepted and signed by A but with the prior agreement of B.

In an overt partnership the approach is somewhat different:

a) A and B would jointly negotiate with the customer.

b) A and B would jointly review and comment on the draft contract.

c) Performance of the contract would rest with them both.

d) The contract would be jointly accepted and signed by A and B.

The third option is for A and B to create an entirely new company on a joint venture basis whose sole purpose would be to execute the one project (or series of projects) with the customer and would thus negotiate and sign the contract with the customer in the normal way. The JVC may be constituted with the minimum assets and staff and, hence, the JVC may then need to place orders with A and B for further goods or services as the diagram shows.

The choice of approach needs careful thought and the extent to which the parties actually 'trust' each other needs to be considered in the context of their partnership contracting agreement. While overt partnership or JVC may suit their wishes neither may be liked by the customer: the former because the customer may prefer to avoid the confusion of signing with two companies, it being easier perhaps to sue only one company if it all goes wrong, and the latter because the customer may judge the JVC to be too relatively insubstantial to carry the burden of his project. However, he may be prepared to accept this if his risk is mitigated by A and B and/or a third party, such as a bank providing a financial guarantee of performance.

A potential pitfall for the parties in both covert and overt partnerships is that a clear definition is still required as to the parts of the work which each will do. Once that is done it tends to drag the relationship back towards conventional arm's length, under which a failure by one party could lead to a claim against it by the other party in respect of delay and additional cost. To avoid this the parties may decide in their partnership contracting agreement to agree to waive all such claims against each other. This certainly motivates them to work together as though they were a single company, but it is a very big decision for each to make and hence the reference to the degree of mutual trust. The good thing about a conventional contract is that it is fairly straightforward to establish liability and remedy if things go wrong. It is less than easy to legislate for the difficult times when the whole premise is mutual success. Rather like those who seek a divorce settlement agreement as part of the contract of marriage, the very act of talking about possible problems can introduce uncertainty in the first place. However, this threat of loss of confidence, like any other risk, is there to be overcome and is not in itself a reason not to proceed.

It should also be borne in mind that both parties may see disadvantage as well as advantage in moving into partnership contracting (Figure 1.10).

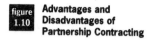

figure 1.10 Advantages and Disadvantages of Partnership Contracting

	Advantages	**Disadvantages**
A	Risk Sharing More Status	Loss of Status
B	Involved in control, management and decision making	Less Control More Risk

Partnership contracting is fairly novel, involves a high level of mutual trust and commitment and demands some big decisions of principle. Nevertheless, it is a sound, productive approach for major, high risk projects.

7 Exclusion clauses

Returning from the sublime considerations of partnership contracting to the conventional contract between buyer and seller, it is necessary to examine one of the blunter instruments of commercial risk management: the use of exclusion clauses to limit or exempt one party from a liability which might otherwise fall to it.

The basic source of authority on such matters is the Unfair Contract Terms Act 1977, which prevents the exclusion of liability for personal injury or death arising from negligence in all forms of contract. However, in non-consumer contracts the parties are allowed to exclude the following subject to a test of reasonableness:

a) Liability for breach of contract.
b) Liability to perform as expected.
c) Liability for complete performance.
d) Liability for other results of negligence.
e) That the goods correspond with description or sample given.
f) Satisfactory quality.
g) Fitness for purpose.

The seller is also prevented from excluding the implied conditions that the goods are unencumbered and that the seller is free to sell them.

The onus is on the party relying on the clause to exclude liability to show that it is reasonable. The reasonableness test is based on:

a) The exclusion being fair and reasonable in the circumstances known or contemplated by the parties when the contract was made.
b) The relative bargaining positions.
c) The existence of any inducement.
d) Whether goods were manufactured, processed or adapted to order.
e) Whether the buyer had reasonable notice of the condition.

If the liability is financially limited then also taken into account would be the resources available to meet the liability and the availability of insurance.

For an exclusion clause to be effective, then:

a) Notice of the clause must have been given at the time of the contract unless the prior course of dealings or trade practice provide evidence of its existence.
b) Notice must be in a contractual document.
c) Reasonable notice must be given.
d) The clause must apply to that which was intended.

In practice it can generally be assumed that in any business contract that is negotiated (ie as opposed to blind acceptance of a standard form contract), the above provisos regarding notice would be deemed satisfied.

An inducement from seller to buyer to accept an exclusion clause may simply be a discount on price. All risks have at least a notional value and the device of an exclusion clause just moves a risk around. If there is valuable consideration, then it should be reasonable that if the buyer has the benefit of a lower price he should not later be able to avoid the exclusion clause under one or more of the foregoing rules.

Frequently it is the satisfactory quality and fitness for purpose undertakings implied (unless they are expressly excluded) by the Sale of Goods Act which suppliers seek to exclude. The argument is that these were intended principally to protect the consumer who buys on the basis of seeing the goods on a shelf, unlike the business purchaser who is 'intelligent' in the sense that he specifies his needs in detail and conducts a thorough appraisal of the utility of the goods before commitment. In such a situation why should the seller carry the imprecise (in scope, extent and time) liabilities of these undertakings? The seller will aim to include clauses such as the following:

'All representations, warranties, guarantees and conditions (other than as to title and those herein expressed or specifically referred to), and whether statutory or otherwise are hereby expressly excluded. Without prejudice to the generality of the foregoing the Company will not be liable for consequential loss or damage, however caused, resulting directly or indirectly from the sale or supply of goods or services by the Company or for any loss or damage caused directly or indirectly by any of the goods or services or in any other way for the performance of any of the goods or services.'

Wow! This is typical of such all embracing clauses which would leave the buyer with very few rights against the seller. Everything from representations made before the contract to problems arising after the contract are excluded from the seller's liability. The courts have been keen to find deficiencies in such clauses so as to preserve natural justice, however, where the clauses have been found legally watertight, then they have been enforced no matter how unreasonable they might seem.

So whether in the role of buyer or seller care should be taken in the use of exclusion clauses as a means of moving risk around.

8. Insurance

Commercial Risk Management is about the allocation of risk between buyer and seller. However, once a particular risk has fallen to one side or the other it does not mean that the carrier has no other option but to hold the risk unto himself. As well as allocating risk the aim is to mitigate risk by passing it on in whole or in part to a third party (Figure 1.11).

figure 1.11 Risk Distribution

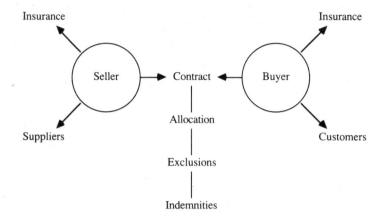

In this chapter so far the idea of using the contract as the vehicle for risk allocation has been explored. Exclusions have been discussed and it should be said that, although certain liabilities cannot be excluded, there is no reason for the party carrying the liability not to be indemnified by the other party regarding the financial consequences of the liability materialising.

In the transaction the seller may seek to distribute his risk amongst his suppliers just as the buyer may attempt to distribute his risk amongst his customers. Nevertheless, both may attempt to lay off some of their respective risks through insurance.

Not all risks inherent in a commercial transaction are insurable. At the heart of such a deal is the prospect of gain for which reason the risk is taken in the first place. If failure of the enterprise were to be insurable as far as the loss of that potential gain is concerned, then there would be no incentive to work to achieve that gain and insurance companies would forever be paying for lost anticipated profits which result from no more than the company failing to strive for that goal. However, if the failure were to result from a fortuitous event (such as fire), then provided there is sufficient number of similar risks to allow a sensible prediction of the loss to be assessed and a reasonable premium to be calculated, then such risk is insurable. For a risk to be insurable the insured must also have an 'insurable interest in the risk'. The Marine Insurance Act 1909 explains this as '(the insured) stands in a legal or equitable relation to the insurable property at risk, in the consequence of which he may benefit by the safety of the property, or may incur a liability in respect thereof.'

For example, company X cannot insure the property of company Y if X stands neither to gain nor lose from the destruction of Y's property.

There are many risks inherent in carrying on any business and those which are insurable include the following:

Type	In respect of
Property	Loss/damage to plant, buildings, materials, stock due to fire, storm, flood etc.
Business interruption	Financial cost of remedial work, new premises, overtime wages etc.
All risks	Property loss/damage not otherwise covered (eg an overseas construction project).
Engineering	For example business disruption due to a computer system failure.
Fidelity guarantee	Theft by employees.
Crime	Theft by third parties.
Product liability	Injury, death or damage caused by defective products.
Public liability	Injury, death or damage to third parties caused by eg the spread of fire.
Director's and officer's liability	Personal liability of directors and officers in respect of business duties.
Goods in transit	Loss or damage to goods while in shipment, whether road, rail, sea or air.
Employer's liability	Injury or death to employees suffered in the course of his employment.
Credit	Customer failure to pay.
Aviation	Injury, death or damage eg caused by aircraft crash resultant from defective equipment.

Many of these are general to the good conduct of the business. Some are required by statute such as public liability and employee liability. Some make good sense such as 'engineering' provided the premium is not excessive in comparison with the perceived potential loss. Some may result from a particular contract. For example, a company supplying for the first time products that will be built into an aircraft should examine the possibility of aviation insurance, especially so if the products are hazardous or critical to aircraft safety. Others such as credit and goods in transit may be geared to one or many contracts.

It is good commercial risk management when identifying the potential risks in a particular deal to consider special insurance, or at the very least to determine whether existing insurance policies cover the appropriate insurable risks in scope and value without unreasonable exclusions applying.

One of the drawbacks of insurance is that once a risk is insured people stop thinking about it and if they think about it at all they tend to dismiss the risk as 'not to worry, it's covered'. As each invitation to tender or contract crops up there are several stages to consider:

a) Review the document, the implications of expressed and implied risks and identify the insurable risks.
b) Check that existing insurance policies cover these risks.
c) Identify additional cover required and ensure that the premium represents value for money against the protection provided.
d) Ensure that the contract price embraces any necessary additional premiums or that their cost is otherwise provided for.
e) Ensure that project and contract managers are aware of the insurance position and in particular that exclusions, limitations and 'excesses' are understood.

Any insurer is only going to pay out if the risk is covered, if the cover is adequate and provided the insured has reasonably acted to prevent or mitigate the effects of the event. In any event, insurance can only provide financial compensation for the event and not for the other consequences to the business. For example, if the company is able to insure against the risk of failure by a key supplier, financial compensation in respect of additional costs or other financial penalties resulting from supplier failure is little help in preventing good customers from going elsewhere. The company should work hard to avoid any risk materialising regardless of whether or not it is insured.

9. Customer characteristics

The whole subject of commercial risk management is about managing the risk that lies across the contractual interface between company and customer, between company and suppliers and embracing the effect of extraneous influences such as 'force majeure' events that intrude into these essentially private arrangements. In the analysis, however, it would be easy to assume that in the crucial contractual interface between Company and Customer all customers are the same. A thorough description of a particular customer would have to include the following:

a)	Status	:	Public or private
b)	Location	:	UK or overseas
c)	Nationality	:	British or foreign
d)	Culture	:	Western or not
e)	Language	:	English or not
f)	Religion	:	Important or not
g)	Size	:	Employees, sites, turnover
h)	Substance	:	Assets, credit status
i)	Reputation	:	Good faith dealings
j)	Procurement policy	:	Strict competition – 'dutch auction' etc
k)	Personnel	:	Quality and integrity

Good customer relations demand that these characteristics are identified, understood and responded to sympathetically by the company, particularly on matters such as culture and religion. However, these considerations are just as essential in risk management as in customer relations. Failure to understand the essence of the customer is to expose unnecessary risks. If the customer says the draft contract will be issued in a week, the company must know whether this means what it says or whether it means that the customer is just stringing the company along while formal negotiations have already opened with the opposition. If the customer says it is contemplating a £50 million contract, the company should know not only that the customer has the money/credit to proceed, but that it has the numbers and quality of personnel to handle a major order and that its approval procedures are of a realistic time frame.

Commercial Risk Management starts with knowing the customer.

0. Company culture

If knowing the customer is important then the culture and organisation of the company is paramount if risks are to be avoided. Established companies arrive at their organisation not so much by clear design but by evolution, taking into account company, local and national politics (eg setting up operations in areas of high unemployment to attract subsidies and cheap labour), geography (eg the location of customers, suppliers, airports and other communications), different cultures and practices (eg when companies merge or are taken over) and other such diverse and possibly conflicting influences. The net effect can be to produce an organisation which may look sound to the outside world but which at the same time is inherently not optimised for risk management. The manifestation of this phenomenon can be on the macro scale (eg the way in which the company is structured by different operating divisions) and on the micro scale (eg inconsistent procedural arrangements).

Good examples of this type of problem are:

a) **Geographical separation of design and manufacture**
   This produces an 'us and them' attitude. The designers create what they think is a good design and blame the factory for not being able to make it. The factory complains that the design is not geared for manufacture and cannot be made cheaply. The result is a poor, expensive product that is always delivered late.

b) **Functional separation of selling and buying**
   If there is no functional linkage between those responsible for negotiating terms with customers and those responsible for negotiating with suppliers, there is inevitably a mismatch between the respective terms, possibly leaving the company holding a liability which should properly belong to a supplier.

c) Allowing 'non buyers' to buy

To save time and money companies allow personnel who are not expert buyers to purchase apparently innocuous things. Engineers buying software, administration staff buying photocopy services are examples where important commercial and financial issues are overlooked through ignorance.

d) Following a strict 'buy cheap' policy

'Lowest price wins' is not usually the invariable recipe for success if short and long term risk are not considered.

e) Management attitude

The concept of Total Quality Management (TQM) teaches that everybody should aim to:

a) Do things right first time.
b) Make sure only the right things are done.
c) Challenge the way things are done.

And yet the single biggest problem is to get senior management away from the idea that 'everything we do is right, it's all those other people who are fouling up'.

If TQM is a sound philosophy (which it undoubtedly is) then it should be backed by a Total Risk Management (TRM) culture. The TQM company takes care over everything that it does. The TRM company goes further and ensures at all stages of its commercial operation that:

a) Risks are identified.
b) Risks are 'owned' (ie allocated to individuals).
c) Risk are avoided, delegated, shared, insured.
d) Risks are mitigated by pro-active management.

Achieving TRM means the company must be prepared to alter its organisation and culture in order to put the necessary facilities and disciplines in place.

Risk analysis
and management

1 Risk

Risk is the possibility that things will not turn out as desired. Thus, in the day to day operation of the business there must be points at which a stand-off view should be taken to assess the current possibility of things going awry. The key points are:

a) Bid/no bid decision · : What is the probability of submitting the winning bid?

b) Tender preparation : What is the probability that the emerging risks can be contained?

c) Contract negotiation : What is the probability of securing a 'safe' deal?

d) Contract performance: What is the probability of completing the contract on time, to specification and within budget?

Each of these topics is addressed in detail elsewhere in other chapters and, of course, it must be said that these points are not really discrete and the questions asked are not really independent. At the outset it would be foolish to ignore the tail end risks. The probability of winning the contract could be 100 per cent if the company offers twice the performance in half the time and at a quarter of the cost as compared with competition. This win-at-all-costs strategy may be good for short-term survival but if it entirely ignores the difficulties of actually achieving what has been promised, then it is nothing more than a recipe for certain eventual disaster.

Every type of risk has a potential adverse risk on

Cost	–	the cost budget fixed for undertaking the work may be exceeded reducing the margin for profit.
Time	–	the ability to complete the contract in accordance with the dates or schedule dictated thereby may be prejudiced.
Performance	–	the ability to deliver fully in conformance with mandated specifications and standards may be affected.

The sources of these risks tend to lie in one of four areas:

Source		**Examples**
Customer	–	geographically remote
	–	poor credit standing
Subcontractors/	–	different priorities
Suppliers	–	technical competence
Third parties	–	regulatory bodies
	–	patent infringement
In-house	–	'risk naive' organisation
	–	under-resourcing

These examples neatly indicate that any contract is beset by risks which are both technical and commercial in character. Although appraisal of risk in the technical arena is very important, it is equally as important to consider the other half of the equation:

2 Benefits

So if the potential benefits are the heightened prospect of pleasing company, customer and shareholders, then the realisation of these benefits is achieved through:

a) Learning from mistakes.
b) Ensuring that potential problems are exposed and given proper visibility.
c) Company and customer being realistic about cost, time and performance.
d) Promoting a relationship-based transaction.
e) Improved decision making.

There is unfortunately nothing quite like a significant project failure to instil in people a real view of how things can and do go wrong. There is nothing new about learning from experience and yet too frequently a company can fail to draw on lessons that should have been learnt in undertaking its risk analysis for the next major bid. Once a major project is up and running it tends to become a mini company within the company. It has its own management, reporting, procedures and culture, one characteristic of which is to keep its problems to itself. There can be an unwillingness to open the barriers and draw in new ideas or experience from the outside, but at the same time there is no transmission out to the rest of the business of problems suffered, solutions found and consequences encountered. And yet this should be a real source of data for the risk analysis of the next prospect.

Once risk analysis has brought potential problems out into the open it is vital for senior management within the company to be aware, to react and to support the necessary counter-measures. Senior management is the internal customer to whom the project/contract manager must 'deliver' happy customers and lots of profit. Senior management, rather like external customers, does not like 'surprises'. A sudden adverse impact on the anticipated project profit caused by the manifestation of a risk that could and should have been exposed at the bid/no bid or contract award stage is unforgivable.

Most importantly, if the topic of risk and its impact on cost, time and performance can be drawn into open discussion with the customer, then inherently there will be a greater sense of realism. The customer must acknowledge at this stage that the level of risk and where the risk lies are quite distinct and separate issues and the latter should not be allowed to cloud or influence the view of the former. For example, to leave the cost risk with the company by the use of firm price tendering, or to leave the schedule risk with the company by contractual deadlines 'backed up' by Liquidated Damages, do not of themselves have any significant impact on the intrinsic risk to the success of the project. It is right for the customer to attempt to avoid the contractual liability for project failure, but all the contractual penalties on the company in the world cannot make the project a success if it is founded upon a flawed view of the real-world risk. Much better for both sides to be honest, realistic and to operate on a partnership basis than to pretend everything is all right, relying on the lawyers to earn their keep later. However, both sides will nevertheless have a weather eye on the extent of their contractual liability within whatever framework upon which they have settled, and each will carefully seek to avoid prejudicing its position through the process of mutual risk management.

The proper use of risk analysis at the earliest stages also improves decision making as the fullest of information is available. To this extent perhaps organisations have always undertaken risk analysis and some might say that any proposal or presentation to the company that invited a major decision (eg to bid, to accept a contract, to make a capital investment) was wholly inadequate if it failed to draw attention to the risks as well as the benefits. However, formal risk analysis has two distinct advantages. Firstly, because it is formal, it is thorough and highly disciplined. Thus more risks are identified at any earlier stage. Secondly, because it includes planning and management (of the risks, rather than of the project), it ensures that there will be little chance of surprises and for every adverse event there is a pre-planned contingency plan which can be quickly and smoothly brought into play.

2. Bid and project risk management – an important distinction

Before this appraisal of the techniques of risk analysis and management goes too far it is important to highlight a distinction between risk management at the bid stage and risk management at the project stage. Firstly, returning to the four risk review points mentioned at the beginning of this chapter, a different complexion can be placed (Figure 2.1).

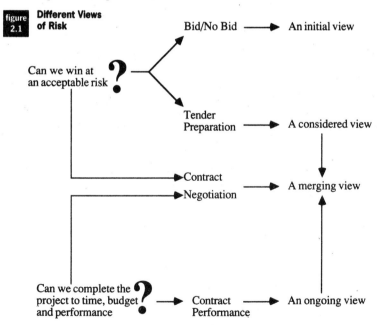

figure 2.1 Different Views of Risk

Although there is an overlap between them the two questions 'Can we win?' 'Can we perform?' are in essence quite different in character. A mistake that is sometimes made is to undertake risk analysis during the bid stage only in respect of the second question. This is to deny to the fundamentally important first question the benefits of formal risk analysis and risk management.

Consider these issues presented somewhat differently (Figure 2.2):

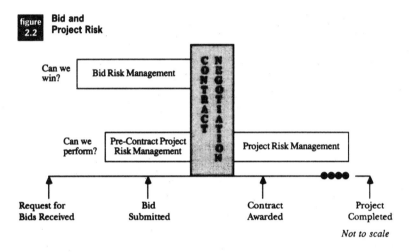

figure 2.2 **Bid and Project Risk**

Not to scale

In the pre-contract stage two risk management activities should be underway. One looks at the problems associated with preparing an attractive bid on time and defeating the opposition. The other is concerned with predicting if the project can be completed successfully. Naturally, if the early work on the latter question produces a very high probability of failure then that result could have a devastating effect on the desire to bid and Bid Risk Management would become superfluous.

However, at this stage it is sufficient to have outlined the distinction between bid risk and project risk management. The succeeding paragraphs look at the techniques of risk analysis and management and then the two areas of risk management will be reviewed to establish the applicability to each of those techniques.

 # Phases of risk management

Risk Management includes five primary phases:

Phase 1:	Identification	–	Sources
		–	Areas
		–	Inter-dependencies
Phase 2:	Initial Analysis	–	Listing and Ranking
		–	Probability and Impact
Phase 3:	Modelling	–	Statistical Techniques
Phase 4:	Planning	–	Mitigation Options
		–	Fall-back Plans
Phase 5:	Management	–	Tracking and Review
		–	Fall-back Implementation
		–	Replanning

To describe these as phases is slightly misleading as it implies seriality. In fact once analysis or planning has started it does not mean that identification must cease. Handling risk is a highly dynamic process which involves not only the management of previously known risks but also reacting effectively to an evolving situation. When Montgomery fought the battle of Normandy, history criticised him for constantly maintaining that everything had gone according to plan. In reality he reacted dynamically (or as dynamically as heavy rain and mud allow) to a changing tactical situation as known risks were contained and new ones emerged. Total Risk Management in the business world is remarkably similar, demanding not only constant review and a capacity to react quickly and effectively against a new situation, but also a willingness to ensure that the changing position and the countermeasures proposed have appropriate visibility within the company.

5. Risk identification

Clearly the beginning of the identification phase is the crucial starting point from which a thorough and comprehensive search must be done to discover all sources (eg subcontractors) and areas (eg system design) of risk. At this qualitative stage the three best techniques for flushing out risk are:

1) Brainstorming
2) Interviewing
3) Drawing on existing risk database.

These three techniques are quite different in nature (Figure 2.3) and as such should provide a wide coverage in the search for risk.

figure 2.3 Risk Identification Techniques

	Nature	Skill Demanded
Brainstorming	Active predictive	Analytical, conceptual
Interviewing	Passive predictive	Probing, exploratory
Existing Database	Passive historic	Insight

Brainstorming should take place at all levels to drive out all the imponderable 'what ifs'. This is just as important at the strategic level (eg what happens to overhead rates on this contract if business volume declines elsewhere while this project is underway) as it is in the technical forum on the particular contract. In brainstorming the emphasis is very much on the brainstormers producing their own ideas of where risk might lie. By contrast the interviewing technique relies heavily on the skill of the interviewer in questioning managers, engineers, technicians, etc, as to the possibility of risk existing in the areas for which they were individually responsible. It is surprising how often people will give the knee jerk reaction that 'there is no risk in my area' (perhaps to avoid the impression of being a poor manager), only to agree upon being interviewed that not all is as safe as it seems. On the other hand the individual who confesses to high risk, perhaps because of an ulterior motive (eg to gain a bigger budget), may find upon careful questioning that the risk is not so great after all.

Comparing these predictive views of risks with real events on an historic database is a good way of both validating the magnitude of the perceived view and of double-checking that no category or type of risk has been accidentally omitted from the brainstorming and interview processes.

As an essential ingredient of the identification phase it is important to establish which risks are independent and which are inter-dependant. Clearly a series of risks which all lie on the critical path (Figure 2.4) cannot be considered individually in isolation as their combined effect following the 'domino' principle could be catastrophic.

figure 2.4 Critical Path

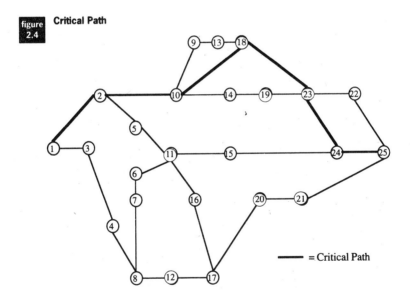

━━━ = Critical Path

The approach to risk identification must be structured and comprehensive and can be extracted from a combination of the management organisation and work breakdown structures (Figure 2.5).

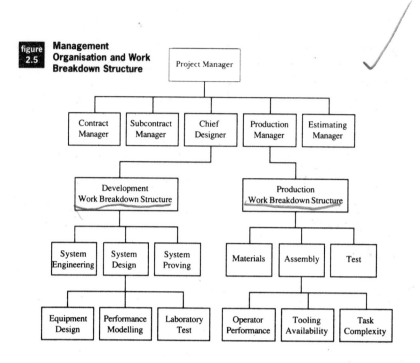

figure 2.5 Management Organisation and Work Breakdown Structure

This highly stylised diagram shows that every function within the business and every task covered by the project is a potential source of risk. Thus, whether individuals are business function oriented or project task oriented, everyone has a role to play in the process of identifying risk.

6. Analysis

In fact the diagram shown at Figure 2.5 may not be comprehensive enough to capture all the potential sources of risk. One of the golden rules of risk analysis is to keep a broad perspective and avoid the 'cannot see the wood for the trees' syndrome.

Thus while the final project risk model may have hundreds of individual activities, it is important to start out at the macro level, for which it is necessary to return to the primary sources of risk mentioned earlier. In the example of a major building project the most significant areas of risk may be as shown in Figures 2.6 and 2.7.

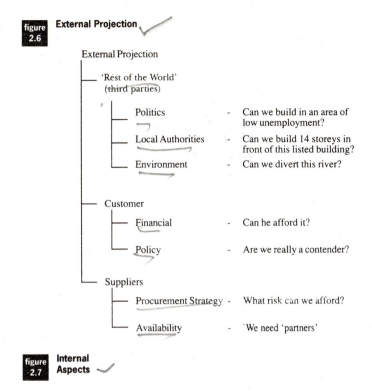

figure 2.6 **External Projection**

External Projection

    'Rest of the World'
    (third parties)

        Politics   -   Can we build in an area of
                                low unemployment?

        Local Authorities   -   Can we build 14 storeys in
                                front of this listed building?

        Environment   -   Can we divert this river?

    Customer

        Financial   -   Can he afford it?

        Policy   -   Are we really a contender?

    Suppliers

        Procurement Strategy - What risk can we afford?

        Availability   -   'We need 'partners'

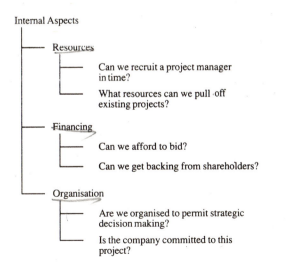

figure 2.7 **Internal Aspects**

Internal Aspects

    Resources

            Can we recruit a project manager
            in time?

            What resources can we pull off
            existing projects?

    Financing

            Can we afford to bid?

            Can we get backing from shareholders?

    Organisation

            Are we organised to permit strategic
            decision making?

            Is the company committed to this
            project?

An important step in the whole process is to list the most significant risks and set them in an order of ranking.

This can be converted into a risk map (Figure 2.8) to give an overall impression of where attention most needs to be concentrated.

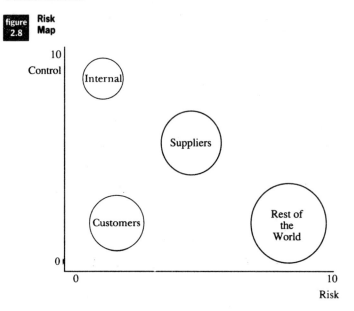

figure 2.8 Risk Map

The objective is to have small 'bubbles' all hovering near to the (0,10) coordinate. All the macro risks in each of the four zones should either be in or very close to the category of 'if we can't resolve this risk then we won't go ahead'. In this way, early decision making focuses on the really important principles and avoids nugatory time and effort being spent on a prospect which might otherwise prove to be too risky or futile.

The next step in the initial analysis is to take each risk and assess the probability of the risk arising and the impact of the risk should it materialise. This provides the means to create a risk grid (Figure 2.9).

Risk Grid

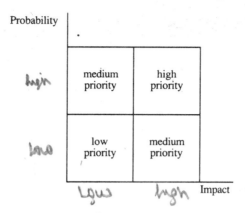

Thus, the discipline of causing individuals to identify all risks and to consider both the impact and probability of each specific risk, helps to point out where attention most needs to be directed.

7 Modelling

In simple terms a risk potentially impacts upon cost, time or performance or combinations thereof. The question then arises as to whether it is possible to produce an accurate prediction, for example, as to the cumulative net effect of all the risks that may affect time. Such a quantative process would provide further insight beyond the qualitative stages of assessing impact for individual risks at the crude level of high, medium or low.

The combination of statistical techniques and computer processing power has allowed the development of commercially available risk modelling packages that provide just this sort of prediction. It is at the highly detailed level that these techniques produce the most useful result. For example, in a large project for which detailed activity planning is done, the overall plan may have thousands of discrete activities, each of which has a potentially variable duration depending upon its level of complexity as well as its intrinsic size. The modelling process requires that the engineers (or other personnel as appropriate) responsible for producing the time estimates for those activities are required to generate so-called 'three point estimates' rather than a single estimate for each activity. The three points are worst case, best case and most likely. One or more of the following probability range is then assumed for each of the three point estimates:

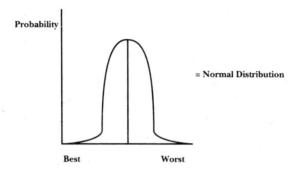

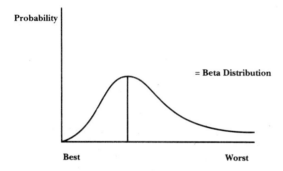

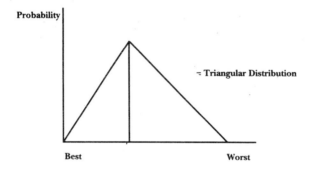

In each of the three diagrams the vertical line shown indicates the 'most likely' outcome. Normal distribution assumes that the best case is as likely as the worst case, with the probability remaining symmetrical either side of the most likely point. Beta and triangular distributions both skew the probability distribution towards the worst case. That is to say that overall it is more likely that things will turn out worse than the perceived most likely outcome. Real world experience instinctively indicates this to be the case. For example, a golfer asked to say how many shots he would take on a par 4 hole might say that his most likely outcome would be five shots, at worst ten and at best a hole in one. Clearly the best case can be no better than one whereas it is feasible for the worst case to exceed ten.

Having gathered and entered this data into the computer model the analysis is then done with the computer taking each activity and sampling the likely outcome from somewhere within the probability distribution envelope. This produces an overall probability distribution (Figure 2.10) for the entire project.

figure 2.10 **Project Time Frame Probability Distribution**

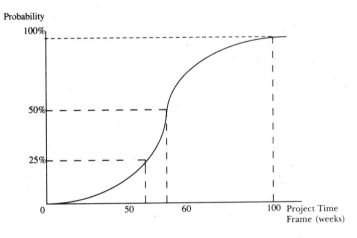

A probability curve of this shape indicates only a 50 per cent chance of completing within 60 weeks, a 25 per cent chance of completing within 50 weeks but a 100 per cent chance of completing within 100 weeks. If the customer requires, say, 55 weeks, this is bad news! If he can wait 95 weeks then time frame is not a problem.

The model can be run several times on each occasion, sampling at different points within the individual activity probability frequency distributions. This produces a series of similar curves (**Figure 2.11**).

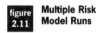

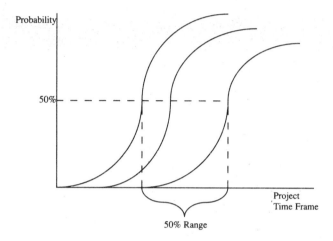

50% Range

Multiple runs of the model produce a further refinement of the likelihood of hitting a particular time frame.

The usefulness and reliability of the results depend on a number of things including the number of activities for which three point estimates are produced, the care taken in producing those estimates, the number of times those estimates are updated, the choice of triangular or beta distributions and, indeed, the particular modelling package.

Planning and management

The final phases of risk management involve establishing specific plans to mitigate the risks and, most importantly, the identification of fall-back plans and the dates by which those plans must be implemented. The management of risk demands the active process of regular risk reviews and the commitment to actually enact the fall-back plan and adopt its deadline. The situation must not be allowed to drift so that deadlines pass and no positive action is taken.

Essentially the action to mitigate a risk can either be a 'passive' one, in which the mitigation action is only taken once the risk has materialised, or it can be an 'active' one in which early steps are taken to ensure that if the risk does materialise then its impact is much reduced or effectively eliminated entirely. Inevitably any action taken to mitigate the effect of a risk has a cost associated with it. Thus an active mitigation action may have an 'upfront' cost which may be a prudent investment to make or it may prove to be an unnecessary expenditure. For example, building a road tunnel which needs the fabrication of a special tunneling machine runs the risk that the work will be delayed if that unique machine breaks down. Clearly the passive risk mitigation strategy would be to repair the machine if it breaks.

The active strategy might be to fabricate a second 'back-up' machine at the outset. If the primary machine does not fail the money will have been wasted; if it does break the back up will be invaluable. Clearly the choice between active and passive strategies requires a careful cost benefit analysis. In the example given the passive strategy would be preferable if the cost of the second machine is greater than the likely cost of delay, or indeed greater than the cost of insuring against the consequences of delay.

An essential ingredient of risk management is that every risk should be allocated to an individual person or 'owner'. There needs to be individual responsibility even if the actual management or mitigation demands a team effort. Similarly, risk management should be seen as an integral part of business management. It is simply another tool which should be used as part of the day-to-day running of the company. For example, risk management should be seen as part of project management and not a separate 'off line' activity albeit that the project manager may draw upon a risk management source of expertise, just as he might draw upon specialists in estimating or quality assurance.

The Risk Register

The repository for all risks should be the Risk Register (Figure 2.12). This provides the essential reporting and control medium which should be updated and reviewed on a regular basis. For the purposes of clarity and focus there should be two Risk Registers. The first is for Bid Risk Management and the second for Project Risk Management.

figure 2.12 Risk Register

Serial	Risk	Owner	Probability	Impact C T P O I E S M R T E F	Mitigation Plan	Fall-back Plan	Fall-back Deadline

The Risk Register, or Risk Log, draws together in one place all the principles of sound risk management:

- Identification
- Ownership
- Probability
- Impact
- Mitigation
- Fall-back

10. Applicability

Without any doubt at all the formality and disciplined approach of risk analysis and management is highly applicable and beneficial to both Bid Risk Management and Project Risk Management. The completion of the Risk Register is a major step in achieving an understanding of what is involved in bidding and performing the potential contract. On the other hand, the use of risk modelling based on three point estimates has its best application in Project Risk Analysis, where there is a real need to apply statistical predictive techniques to the huge volume of activities that arise in a major project. This is not to say that risk analysis and management should not be applied to small bids, contracts or projects. It should become a way of life to use these ideas on all enterprises, although clearly the degree of application will vary according to the scale of the enterprise.

Returning to the distinction between Bid Risk Management and Project Risk Management, the different nature of the risks in each can be seen in the following example:

Bid Risk Management	Project Risk Management
■ Customer favours existing supplier	■ Very high software content
■ Competitors may bid low cost non-compliant solutions	■ New processor chips won't be available on time
■ Our teaming partner may be acquired by a competitor	■ Programme time frame allows too little time for system integration
■ Customer may demand company contribution to contract costs	■ Specification tolerances very tight

This puts the two categories of risk management into perspective. The establishment of the risk register for the bid provides a basis for qualitative management decision making in terms of bid strategy. It would be difficult to see how risk modelling (in the sense of the application of mathematical, statistical techniques) could sensibly be applied. 'Modelling' in the sense of working out permutations of events and playing 'what if' scenarios is useful. Qualitative management decision making is also important for the project but statistical modelling clearly has a role to play on issues such as the programme time frame.

Indeed, since it is suggested that risk management techniques are simply an additional tool to assist in business planning and management, these applications can be seen as part of larger processes (Figure 2.13).

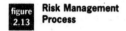

Risk Management Process

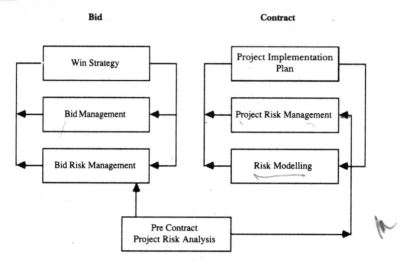

The purpose of this chapter has been briefly to explain what is meant by risk analysis and management in a formal sense, to show that there are, broadly speaking, two risk dimensions ('technical' and 'commercial') and that application for the techniques can be found in both the bid and project stages. For those interested in studying the techniques and the mathematics of risk modelling, particularly with regard to the technical dimensions, there are many good sources for further reading. The remainder of this book concentrates on the commercial dimension.

3

Pre-contract risk

1 The risk–risk scenario

Bidding for a contract involves a twin risk. Firstly, there is the risk of losing the competition and, secondly, there is the risk of winning it! As a cynic might say, 'the good news is that we've won the competition, the bad news is that now we have got to perform the contract'. In any competition for business there is the risk that the prize turns out to be a lemon. A lemon contract is one which turns out to be more costly to perform than anticipated, or one where the other expected fruits of the enterprise turn sour. The contract that is delivered late incurs customer displeasure and loss of reputation. The contract that was anticipated to take the company into new technologies or to address additional markets, but leads only into a blind alley nugatorily diverting time, cost and effort can be a commercial disaster.

In the previous chapter a simple distinction was made between Bid Risk Management and Project Risk Management. In this chapter the process of moving through evolving bid risk management into a 'no turning back' decision and then on into an effective 'risk understood' contract will be explored.

2 Deciding to bid

Making a decision to bid for a significant contract is a major step.

Once the decision has been made the bid gains a momentum and almost a personality of its own. Once it is thundering along it can be almost impossible to stop. The risk that is taken at this early stage is gambling the cost of bidding against the chances of winning. The cost of bidding is more than just the money spent:

- Diversion of resources
- Not bidding other contracts
- Reputation of the bid manager
- Reputation of the company

Money spent on one bid means that money is not available for bidding other contracts. Bidding soaks up valuable resources as the company, not unnaturally, wishes to put its best people on to bidding for an important new piece of work. Many companies do not have the luxury of maintaining top teams whose task is exclusively bidding. Indeed, such dedication may in itself be a risk in so far as bid preparation by people not involved in contract execution lacks that vital element of experience, the absence of which either makes the bid of academic interest only to the customer or some key activity or risk is missed in the costing/pricing exercise. Thus the best source, and possibly the only source, of expert people for the bid team is current contract work where the diversion of key people may introduce additional risk, cost and possibly delay to that work. Once the bid is underway it becomes a personal challenge, and rightly so, for the bid manager to submit the bid no matter what and, of course, to win the contract. Similarly, the company, in its dealings with the customer and with potential suppliers, is keen to show that it can submit an attractive bid. Again, this is rightly so but the point is that once bid preparation is in hand no one wants to stop it for fear of loss of face, writing off nugatory expenditure and losing the chance of winning. This means that the decision to bid in the first place must be a good decision.

Risk analysis of the prospects of winning and risk analysis of the potential contract must begin very early on and be maintained throughout. Certainly the prospects of winning can alter as the bid phase proceeds and more information or intelligence becomes available. News that an arch competitor has a new product available, news that an overseas bidder has support from his own government in making a subsidised bid, news that the company has become unpopular with the customer – all might indicate that the prospects of winning have slumped. These things do happen and so bid strategy should be based upon:

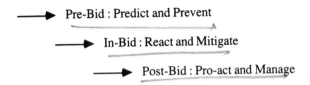

⟶ Pre-Bid : Predict and Prevent

⟶ In-Bid : React and Mitigate

⟶ Post-Bid : Pro-act and Manage

In the examples given it might be possible to predict the possibility of an overseas subsidised bid and prevent it by political lobbying. If the company is rumoured to be unpopular (eg because of problems on a current contract), then it should react and take extraordinary steps to mitigate whatever the problem might be before the customer develops a 'mind set', in which the perception of the company's alleged poor performance becomes absolutely fixed. If, after the bids are submitted, a competitor is discovered to have unexpectedly offered a new product, the company may try 'spoiling' tactics by attempting to 'rubbish' that new product in the customer's eyes by drawing his attention to the unproven and hence high risk nature of that product.

In the extreme a continuing risk analysis (of the probability of winning) as bid preparation proceeds might lead to a conclusion that, whereas at the outset the chances of winning were estimated at a certain level, the unfolding of events and the gaining of intelligence during the bid alters that initial perception (Figure 3.1).

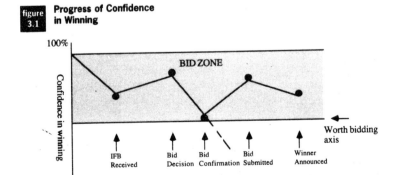

figure 3.1 **Progress of Confidence in Winning**

Figure 3.1 gives a not untypical view of the progress of the confidence level in submitting the winning bid:

Pre-IFB : Before receiving the Invitation For Bids (IFB), early confidence may be very high because the initial intelligence is that the company is the market leader, the 'sitting' supplier and traditionally the most competitive on price. Confidence may wane as, perhaps, discussions with the customer show he is keen to encourage new, innovative solutions to his requirements.

IFB received : On receipt of the IFB, confidence recovers as it is realised that the IFB is 'written around' the company's product. So a decision to bid is made.

Post decision to bid : Again confidence wanes as the enormity of the requirement, lack of adequate bid preparation time, scarcity of top team bid people all strike home.

Bid submitted : As the bid is submitted, confidence level is high as the bid team congratulates itself on completing the bid and getting it submitted on time.

However, the company should be clear at what level of confidence it is worth bidding. If ongoing risk analysis shows the confidence level (the dotted line on Figure 3.1) falling through the Worth Bidding Axis, then there should be a serious reappraisal of the prospects and, if action taken does not stop the rot, a decision to withdraw should seriously be considered. Bid reappraisal/ confirmation points should be built into the bid plan at least as far as two thirds of the way through the bidding period. After two thirds most of the bidding cost may have been incurred and it may be as well to finish the bid, even if confidence is low. Before the two thirds point the options are greater. Indeed, it is possible to postulate a 'Rule of Thirds' (Figure 3.2).

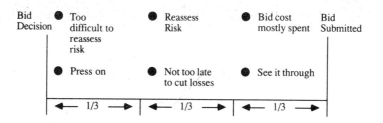

figure 3.2 Risk Reassessment – the 'Rule of Thirds'

In the first period, unless some fundamental, catastrophic event occurs, any risk reassessment would be too uncertain to allow a positive decision to stop the bid. It is only really in the middle period when a more objective reassessment is possible, and while sufficient time and unspent bid cost remains to make a reversal of the bid decision a possibly wise choice.

In deciding to bid, the following risks need to be considered and reassessed as events unfold:

Competitors
- How do their products compare with ours?
- How do their prices compare with ours?
- What is their delivery performance like?
- Do they offer long-term product support?
- What standing/influence do they have with the customer?
- What pricing strategy will they follow (eg 'loss leading')?
- Is there a 'sitting contractor'?

The Requirement
- How complex?
- Are we familiar with it?
- Can we offer compliancy on technical features?

Bidding Resources
- Do we have top team people available to produce the bid?
- Have we got the money to bid?

Partners	– Do we want to bid in a team?
	– If so do we lead?
	– Is there enough time to put a teaming agreement in place?
	– Can/will team members defect to the opposition?
Suppliers	– Do we need any?
	– Are they single source?
	– Do we have time to get and negotiate formal proposals?
Contract Award	– What validity must we offer?
	– How does this fit in with our long-term resource plan?
Contract Conditions	– Can we/dare we reject or comment on the terms and conditions?
	– What risks do they contain?

It can be seen that there are very many things to consider and in terms of those risks which are not associated so much with the process of bidding, but more to do with the potential contract, it is essential to have a strategy for dealing with all such risks. The choices may be:

1) Ignore the risk and hope it does not materialise.
2) Comment on it at the bid stage.
3) Remain silent at the bid stage but aim to deal with it at the contract negotiations.
4) Remain silent at bid and contract negotiation stages but have a plan to eliminate or transfer the risk once in contract.

Ignoring the risk is not an option! Of the other choices the best approach is not always obvious. Commenting on a risk at the bid stage is theoretically the right thing to do because it exposes the issue early on and shows the customer how thoroughly the company has understood the potential contract, and the lengths to which it has gone to respond realistically. On the other hand, it may count against the company when the customer adjudicates all the bids. To eliminate the risk of a caveat against the potential contract, prejudicing the adjudication, it can be as well not to mention the issue until the process is sufficiently well advanced for contract negotiations to have started. The danger here is that a good opportunity may not present itself or that the customer may not entertain new things being introduced at that stage. In this latter situation the risk is that introducing new things may at best irritate a friendly customer or at worst cause him to re-open the competition. This leaves the final choice which is to say nothing until the contract is awarded and underway, when raising the issue, with the intent perhaps of renegotiating the contract, may meet a stone wall or a penalty of some sort.

For example, if a company considers bidding for a contract, knowing or believing it could not meet the delivery requirement, it has a number of choices:

1) No bid.
2) Offer an alternative delivery.
3) Bid to meet the delivery date but aim to shift the date in contract negotiations, perhaps by offering something in return.
4) Bid to meet the delivery date but plan to 'manage' the problem away by finding some excuse of contractual effect.

Not bidding is for the non-gambler. Bidding an alternative date is for 'honest Joe'. The third option is driven by the 'let's get to the table' philosophy and the final option depends on a hard-nosed approach that is based on the pragmatic premise that pre-contract, while the competition is alive, the customer has the greatest bargaining power, but once the contract is underway the balance of bargaining power shifts to some extent towards the company.

So, risk analysis and the planning of how to deal with risks play a crucial part in the process of deciding to bid or not.

Bidding

Once the decision to bid is made, it having been decided to risk the cost of bidding, diversion of resources etc against the potential benefits of securing the contract, the real risk is that the bid will not be produced in a way that generates an attractive result.

Putting a bid together is like a project in its own right. There is a requirement to meet and a deadline to achieve. The result must be a quality bid, produced within budget and delivered on time. Like any other project, it needs a management team (Figure 3.3) and the disciplines that go with it.

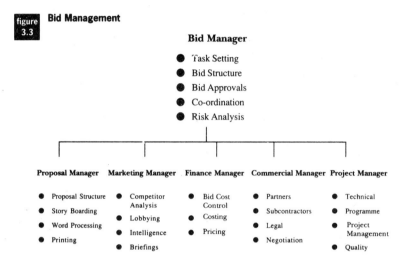

figure 3.3 **Bid Management**

This is a fairly stylised structure but indicates the sort of organisation, functions and responsibilities that can be involved. Its size and constitution will depend on the scale of the bid, but to be successful it will depend upon:

- Having top team experts
- Operating as a tight effective team
- Being dedicated to the bid
- Having the necessary assets and facilities
- Having the necessary finances available

A half-hearted, non-expert, part-time, unfunded team will not produce the winning bid!

As an absolute minimum the project manager must be retained from the bid phase into the contract phase. Ideally, the commercial and finance managers should also be common to both phases. A successful bid put together by these key players will be translated into a major risk to project implementation if there is little or no continuity of personnel between the bid and the contract. This can then become a resource management problem for the company. As has already been said, bid teams need the experience of staff working on contracts and yet, if successful in a new bid, some of those key staff need to move on to the new contract to provide that essential continuity.

An important task for the bid team is to establish a win strategy so that cost and effort can be optimally deployed. The win strategy will always be highly bid specific but must be based on the best intelligence with regard to:

a) Mandatory requirements of the tender invitation.
b) Adjudication procedures.
c) Adjudication criteria.

Additionally, it will include tactics for knocking the opposition and lobbying the customer.

Identifying adjudication criteria is not always easy. Adjudication criteria tend to be formal and published to the bidders, formal but not published, informal (ie invented once bids are received) or absent. If there are no criteria at all then 'lobbying' could well be the principal if not single element to the win strategy. If there are formal, published criteria which include relative weightings between criteria, then a more objective, scientific win strategy can be developed so as to ensure that valuable bid time, money and effort are devoted to those aspects which will win most points in the adjudication.

A good technique for maximising the quality and attractiveness of the bid is to establish a bid 'red team'. The red team's task is not to contribute in any way to the preparation of the bid, but to regularly review the bid during its preparation from the customer's perspective. The characteristics of the red team are:

a) Members must be senior to the bid team members so as to command respect and exercise authority.
b) Disciplines must mirror the disciplines of the customer's adjudication team.
c) Members must know the customer and have the experience

to put themselves in the customer's shoes.

d) Members must have the time and commitment to read and absorb all the bid invitation material and not just 'float around' being clever but disruptive.

e) Members must be hard-nosed and willing to sack members of the bid team or to tell the bid team to tear it up and start again.

The red team has two principal questions to answer. Firstly, it must ensure that the bid is attractive in terms of presentation, content, substance and intelligibility.

It is often the case that bids, certainly the major ones, are comprised of contributions from a wide range and number of sources, possibly including subcontractors or teaming partners. The result can be incoherent and look as though it has been thrown together, even down to relatively minor points such as paper size (EU and US use different standard sizes for example) and character style/font size of typescript. The red team must aim to ensure that the end result is pleasing to the eye and reader friendly.

The second point is whether the bid responds to the questions set by the bid invitation. Bid invitations frequently specify the required structure of bids (eg number of volumes, content of each, number of copies with and without price information), documents to be provided (eg plans and specifications), responses to be given (eg against mandatory features, compliancy matrices) and options to be offered. Bid teams can get carried away doing their own thing. It is the task of the red team to drag the bid team back on to the right path.

4 Pricing for risk

Assuming then that a final, irrevocable decision to bid has been made and assuming that the pre-contract Project Risk Analysis is well established, then a most pressing question arises as to what allowances should be made in the price to cover perceived project risks.

Theoretically, if the price is high enough the company will take any and all risks. However, customers do not have unlimited funds, competition does not permit generous covering of risk within the price and, in any event, a primary obligation of the company is to protect the shareholders' interests and that militates against 'unintelligent' acceptance of untenable or high impact/high probability risks.

If customers can be persuaded to adopt a cost-risk sharing regime (see Chapter 4), so much the better. In such a regime all risks are effectively shared because the immediate risks of performing the contract (eg technical and time frame risks) have, it could be said, no more than a cost impact if they arise. Thus, if costs are shared risk is shared. The remote or consequential risks of performing the contract (eg a third party claiming in respect of personal injury) would not be captured by a cost-risk sharing scheme and still need to be considered regardless of the pricing regime.

If cost-risk sharing is in operation the degree of allowance to build into the scheme (ie the 'width' of the cost incentive range and shape of the curve beyond the two extremes) still needs to be assessed and discussed, but by both sides. However, for the purposes of this chapter it is assumed that cost-risk sharing does not apply and it is for the company alone to determine how to cover risk with regard to prices to be offered.

The primary aim is to keep risk allowances out of the price as any unnecessary allowances merely make the price uncompetitive. To reiterate, it is better to get to the negotiating table with a low price and a game plan to improve the position than to take the safe route of fully pricing for all risks and being eliminated from the competition on the basis of high prices.

Thus, using the pre-contract risk analysis register (see Chapter 2), it should be possible to eliminate certain categories of risk in so far as pricing is concerned:

Category	Risk
1	Risks that can be passed to the customer under the contract.
2	Risks that can be passed to suppliers under the terms of purchase orders and subcontracts.
3	Risks that can be covered by insurance.
4	Risks that ostensibly the company will carry but for which feasible game plans exist to shed the risks if and when they should materialise.

These categories cause very many risks to be excluded. Category 1 risks include such things as passing inflation risk to the customer by including a VOP clause (see Chapter 4) or, for example, passing fitness-for-purpose risk to the customer by using an exclusion clause (see Chapter 1). Category 2 risks may, for example, be eliminating exchange rate risk by paying overseas suppliers in Sterling. In Category 3, insurance will cover costs of delay caused by fire. Liability for lateness in Category 4 might be later transferred to the customer by showing that delay was caused by his acts or omissions.

Thus, attention should be turned to those risks that remain. These can be split into two main headings:

Risk Allowances : Events certain to occur but to an uncertain extent.

Risk Contingency : Events which are uncertain to occur.

The classic example of risk allowance is in a production environment where manufacturing processes always produce a degree of scrap material, rework time and reject rates. However, the degree is variable depending on operator performance, process availability and quality of raw material. A contingent event is one where, for example, although a key supplier has never been late in delivery, it can never be ruled out that one day he might be late.

So, the essential difference between allowances and contingencies is the degree of foreseeability and also that the former will have been experienced before and, hence, existing factual information will exist as the basis for estimating the size of the allowance to include in the price.

Whatever the type of risk, analysis of impact and probability should be carried out (Figure 3.4).

 Impact and Probability

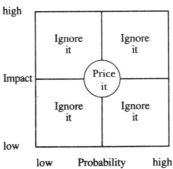

Figure 3.4 shows that many risks are best ignored in so far as pricing is concerned. No risk should be completely ignored but, other than in a cost-risks sharing scheme (see Chapter 4), there is no point covering all the risks by an allowance in the price. Not only would this produce an uncompetitive price but some risks are not appropriate for treatment by pricing allowance. The risk of the contract being cancelled for the convenience of the customer is a serious financial risk but there is little point in putting something in the price for it as, if the contract is cancelled, the price will never be paid as such.

High impact, high probability risks can be ignored because if the impact is high, having a notional value of, say, five times the contract price, then there is absolutely no purpose in including 5 per cent or 10 per cent in the price. Such risks can only be treated in one of two ways. Firstly, by having a game plan to avoid or shed the risk if it arises. Secondly, by deciding not to bid in the first place!

High impact, low probability risks can more safely be ignored. Again there is little purpose putting a nominal risk percentage in the price against a high impact risk which is actually not expected to arise. The strategy should be to ignore it in pricing but keep it under constant review in contract risk management to ensure it does not materialise.

High probability, low impact risks, on the other hand, demand an allowance in the price, but if the impact is very low it is unlikely to be noticeable in the swings and roundabouts of contract performance.

Almost by definition, low probability, low impact risks need not have a pricing allowance made for them.

The foregoing material on pricing for risk has made one implicit assumption. This is that the cost of the job is the subject of sound estimates to which allowances are then added, or not added as the case may be, in relation to identified risks which may later arise, the impact and probability of which have been analysed. However, it is possible that this stable basis may be unstable if the basic cost estimates are wrong, either because of poor estimating or because the job was not understood at the time it was priced. There is little comfort in having done a brilliant analysis of future risks as a result of which 12.75 per cent risk allowance was added to the price if in practice it turns out that the basic costs were underestimated by 5000 per cent! Needless to say, a comprehensive understanding of the prospective job backed up by quality estimating are essential prerequisites to pricing.

One minor complication to be noted in pricing for risk is that some risk allowances should be added to the cost and others added to the price. For example, an allowance for rework can be added to the estimated cost but an allowance for the possibility of the customer claiming liquidated damages should be added to the price in a certain way, if the allowance is to cover the full extent of the liability:

		Method 1		Method 2
Price		100.00		100.00
LD's allowance	x	1.05	÷	0.95
Selling Price		105.00		105.26
Customer charges 5%	x	0.95	x	0.94
Residual Price		99.75		100.00

In this example, where the maximum liability for liquidated damages is 5 per cent, Method 2, which is sometimes referred to as 'on return', results in the full residual price of £100 after the customer actually charges the LD's, whereas Method 1 results in a small shortfall which is an erosion of profit margin.

5. Risk review board

In many companies, when a bid is approved for submission, many people are involved in 'signing it off', but sometimes the approval procedure is excessively concentrated on the price. Such procedures should make it clear that each function within the company is signing for something slightly different. These functions and their responsibilities can be many and varied:

Function	Primarily approves the bid in respect of
Project Manager	■ The entire requirement is understood. Plans and resources exist to discharge the contract.
Technical Manager	■ The technical aspects are understood.
Production Manager	■ The manufacturing requirements are within the company's capability and capacity.
Estimating Manager	■ The requirement has been fully analysed and estimated 'bottom up' using appropriate estimating methods.
Programme Manager	■ Detailed plans exist to show the contract can be completed on time.
Finance Manager	■ Cost estimates and prices have been formulated in accordance with approved rates and factors.
Contracts Manager	■ The terms and conditions have been reviewed and commented upon in line with company policy.
Quality Manager	■ The quality requirements are consistent with company approval.

In addition, those functions which will provide resources in the performance of the contract will:

a) Confirm that resources and their facilities exist or will be brought on-line as the contract demands.

b) Contribute to the cost estimating process and confirm that their responsibilities can be discharged within the costs allowed.

c) Identify any capital expenditure or other investment necessary for the performance of the contract.

The whole bid will be reviewed and authorised with perhaps the final sign off occurring at a 'bid approval' or 'tender vet' meeting.

However, such procedures make the implicit assumption that each function has identified and dealt, in some way or another, with any risks which are associated with their area of responsibility. This type of approach is inadequate as it fails to give risk the necessary exposure in the review-and-approve part of the process.

The procedure should require the establishment of a Risk Review Board whose tasks are:

1) To review, modify if necessary and approve the Pre-Contract Risk Analysis.
2) To interrogate the bid team (see Figure 3.3) or the company functions listed above on the identification of risks in their respective areas and the mitigation plans.
3) To ensure that all risks are 'owned' by an individual.
4) To make the final decision that the risks having been identified, analysed and mitigation planned, result in a net total risk that is acceptable to the company.

These heady responsibilities demand that the Risk Review Board is comprised of senior managers representing the broad perspectives of the company's interests. In particular, the fourth responsibility listed above is most onerous. Companies are in business to make a profit in return for taking a risk, but that does not mean that a company is in business to take any risk, no matter how great, no matter how dire the potential consequences. Therefore, the final decision to proceed or not with the bid must rest with the Risk Review Board un-swayed by the bidding costs incurred, the momentum and wishes of the bid team or the possible reaction of the customer if a bid fails to appear.

Of course the risk–risk scenario demands that initial bid decisions are wise in terms of only bidding those jobs where there is an acceptable probability of winning combined with an anticipation that the resultant potential contract will be 'good business'. Thus the risk-reassessment undertaken during the bid should not only continue to question the probability of winning but, as the pre-contract risk analysis develops, it should also continue to question the attractiveness of that potential contract. No one will thank the bid team for developing a position where there is a 99 per cent probability of winning the greatest lemon in commercial history. Thus, in the normal course of events, bids coming to the Risk Review Board for sanction will be approved but, nevertheless, in performing its duties as Grand High Risk Inquisitor, the Risk Review Board will have made an invaluable contribution to the bidding process.

If, in a conventional bid approval procedure, the emphasis will be on a 'cost and time' consideration, then the extra focus on risk brought about by the Risk Review Board will see different concerns being drawn into the open, for example:

Health and Safety	– Who is signing to say that the products to be offered are free of hazard to life and limb?
Sole Source Suppliers	– What has the purchasing manager done to protect the business against the consequences of default by a sole source supplier?
Customer Financial Status	– What checks have been done on the financial health of the customer?

So the Risk Review Board should draw up a standard pro forma of risks which will form the basis of the pre-contract risk analysis (to which the bid manager would add risks particular to the specific bid) and which it would review as the bid preparation progresses.

6. Making an offer

Having seen preparation of the bid through to its completion and approval, surely there can be no risks associated just with putting the offer on the table? Well, there are eight areas of possible risk:

1) Accidental offers.
2) Validity considerations.
3) Differences between customer and supplier terms.
4) Misrepresentations.

5) Representations.
6) Entirety of the offer.
7) Language.
8) Law.

When the company is ready to make its offer then it should do so by sending its letter, quotation, proposal, bid, tender or by completing the customer's invitation response and, in all cases, marking the bid as a quotation and signed by the company representative having the authority to make formal offers. On the latter point, to the outside world it matters relatively little if the person signing the offer does not actually have the authority of the company, provided that he appears to have. Indeed, it could be said that there is no greater implication of such authority than the act of signing the offer. However, in regular dealings with particular customers, it is good practice for the company to ensure that the customer does know which of its representatives is entitled to sign offers. Furthermore, in the extreme, there is no requirement for offers to be signed by a person provided it is clear that the company is making an offer, albeit that some customers will demand signed offers. The corollary of making it clear that an offer is indeed an offer (ie capable of acceptance in the legal sense) is to make sure that communications with the customer which are not offers per se should be clearly identified so. Letters or other documentation conveying information, outline proposals, indications of cost, budgetary estimates etc should be phrased so that it is clear that no offer is being made. Oral communications should be similarly safeguarded against making an accidental offer.

When an offer is made it is wise to express a validity period. This is the period within which the offer can be accepted so as to create a contract. Unless there is a tender bond, or some valuable consideration for holding the offer open for the stated validity period, then the offer can be withdrawn or amended by the offerer at any time, although to do this during the adjudication of competitive tenders can be risky, unless the customer has called for revised proposals or otherwise allowed adjustments to be made. In any event an offer is effectively cancelled if a counter-offer is made, such as the customer making an offer of contract which is different in some way to the company's offer. The risks in offering a validity period of any significant length are principally twofold. Firstly, that new information will emerge which would cause the company to wish seriously to reconsider its willingness to bid, either in absolute terms or on the basis of the prices or other terms presently on the table. Secondly, there is the problem that the validity required is longer than that offered by the company's suppliers. This risk will have been identified, assessed and allowed for as appropriate in the pricing exercise, but it is nevertheless a good example of the need for careful consideration in offering particular validity periods.

By the time that the offer is submitted to the customer all negotiations with major suppliers should ideally have been completed both as to price and terms, but with the proviso that further negotiations may be necessary as negotiations evolve with the customer. Ideally, those completed negotiations will have produced terms and conditions agreed with suppliers which are no less onerous than those required by the customer, or those upon which the company expects to settle with the customer. The phrase 'no less onerous' is important because it represents the minimum position in terms of holding suppliers on 'back-to-back' terms with the customer's potential contract. For example, if the customer wants twelve months' warranty, then suppliers should be required to give twelve months' warranty. However, while this is strictly back-to-back and no *more* onerous, it leaves the company with the risk of failure of a supplier item which is just outside the supplier's warranty but still within the customer's warranty. Hence the company should seek, say, fifteen months' warranty from the suppliers so as to eliminate its risk in this area. Thus the company can legitimately seek ostensibly more onerous terms from its suppliers. However, the real risk at the point of making the offer to the customer is that those ideals (supplier negotiations complete, no less onerous terms) may not have been achieved. At that stage, actual or anticipated mismatches should have been taken into account either in pricing or in responding to the customer's intended terms. Nevertheless, the risks should be recognised and negotiations with suppliers continued after the offer has been made in order to eliminate or reduce those risks. A danger here is that having failed to achieve the ideals, the supplier's bargaining hand is strengthened if he knows that the offer has been submitted.

Misrepresentations are those inducements to the customer to enter into a contract which are deliberate or innocent mis-representations of factual information. In the extreme the remedy is recession of the contract and liability for damages, plus the possibility of criminal proceedings if the misrepresentation was fraudulent. Thus great care must be exercised in saying and doing things which are intended to persuade the customer to place the contract with the company.

On the other hand, representations are those inducements which are factually correct and which the customer is entitled to believe that he can rely upon, even though the company may not have intended those inducements to form part of his offer or of the consequent contract. If the customer took into account such inducements in making his decision to award the contract, then he can expect them to be implied into the contract even though express terms are absent. Representations can be made quite unintentionally and the risk can be high of undertaking a greater obligation than was intended. Although customers are expected to reasonably distinguish between material which is merely advertising 'puffery' and that which is intended to create a binding obligation, the division between puffery and real intent can be unclear, particularly in matters of technical detail. In the bidding and adjudication process it is common for customers to seek clarifications from companies as to the detail or ambiguities in their individual offerings. Answers given can be the simple clarification sought, or they can possibly create additional obligations, either because a simple, brief answer establishes a broader obligation than that conveyed by the detail of the original technical proposal, or because the company chooses to take advantage of the request for clarification by 'improving' its bid (indeed it may be that that was exactly what the customer was seeking). The case is similar when the customer allows bidders to summarise their offers by giving a presentation of their bids followed by a question and answer session. This is usually a golden opportunity for the company to really 'sell' its offer and yet in enthusiastic, 'Don't worry, we can do it' presentation-speak, representations really can accidentally be made.

The risk of accidental representations can be avoided by including in the contract an 'entire agreement' or 'complete agreement' clause, which details all of the documents which together constitute the whole agreement between the parties. The parties can therefore decide whether the contract is made up only of those contract documents prepared by the customer as a formal offer of contract, or whether the agreement can incorporate by reference earlier material, such as the company's bid, written clarifications, third party specifications and standards. Thus, by expressly stating what is in the agreement, anything else is automatically excluded, including representations (such as those conveyed by presentation visual material, 'hand-outs' etc), which would otherwise be implied into the agreement. The use of entire agreement clauses to exclude what otherwise would have been implied terms is subject to a reasonable test. Preceding the entire agreement clause in the contract, the company should provide an 'entire offer' statement within its bid. For example, the bid may be submitted under a covering letter highlighting the key benefits of the offer written in marketing terms, rather than those of the lawyer. The offer may be bound in several volumes of which one is an 'executive summary', the purpose of which again is to focus on the main advantages of awarding the contract to the particular company. In either case it should be decided whether such summaries are part of the formal offer in the strictest sense. They certainly are part of the proposal but are they intended to be part of the resultant contract? Sometimes the customer may ask for information (eg an analysis of prices, predicted life cycle costs), which is helpful in bid adjudication but which is definitely not intended (by the company at least) to be part of the contract. The discipline of providing an entire offer statement helps the company to be clear in its own mind what exactly it is offering and what it is not. This may lead to the risk of the customer being put off because of the overt exclusions and hence the decision may not be to draw attention to the entire offer statement until contract negotiations are under way!

Finally, there are the issues of the language and applicable law of the contract. In any international contract, the official language of the contract should be stated. All contracts should state the applicable law under which the contract is created and to which it will be performed (these can be different, one law for formation and one for performance and possibly a third for arbitration!). If the language is other than English there is a risk of ambiguity arising in the translation. The converse is true for the non-English speaking customer of course, but since English has become the standard language of commerce, business and industry, the mother tongue is preferable. If the law is other than English Law or Scots Law much uncertainty is introduced as foreign laws can be markedly different from the UK varieties in terms of implied obligations and duties.

Thus the English language and a UK law should be stated as a premise for the bid.

 The priced list of risks

The foregoing shows that the simple act of making an offer can be fraught with risks. Nevertheless, as the bid goes on to the table it represents, amongst other things, a particular set of proposed risk allocations between company and customer. However, there is nothing to prevent and much to commend in the company offering options in terms of allocation of risk. Most risks have a value to the buyer (how much would he pay not to carry a risk) and a value to the seller (how much would he reduce his price to avoid a risk). These values are variable in themselves and may not naturally coincide between company and customer. For example, the company may be prepared to reduce its price by 5 per cent in exchange for the customer carrying the risk of inflation driven cost increases. The customer may be prepared to pay 10 per cent more not to carry that risk. Clearly there is room to negotiate! Such variation in the valuation of particular risks may reflect no more than a differing perception of the probability and impact of the risks. It may reflect the fact that one side may be better able or logically more appropriate to carry the risk. In government contracts it is often argued that the government should carry the risks in inflation cost increases as the level of inflation is a function of the effectiveness of the instruments of government policy.

Emerging from these considerations is the idea that the company could put forward a priced list of risks as options for the customer to consider. All companies are used to offering options in terms of differing quantities, alternative products or performance and varying delivery rates, but the concept of offering risk options is one that should be given some thought. The risk options can be offered with the bid or during contract negotiations, whichever appears the optimum strategy in the given circumstances.

Not only does this approach do full justice to the principle of using the contract as a risk allocation vehicle, but it would also assist in post-contract dispute resolution. For example, if post-delivery liabilities (express warranty, implied warranty, Sale of Goods Act implied undertaking) can be shown to have been discussed in detail pre-contract, with the customer enjoying some financial or other valuable considerations for reducing or eliminating the company's post-delivery liabilities, then the company has a strong and clear case for defending any later action by the customer in the event of a post-delivery problem.

The caveats register

From the point at which the invitation for bids is received through to the moment at which the contract is signed, the very many people involved in bid preparation and in the planning of contract execution regularly identify issues associated with the potential contract. Some of these issues may be so important that they must be identified at the time of bidding. Some may be less critical and can be left until contract negotiations. Some may be minor issues to do with the terms and conditions, others may be fundamental premises upon which the price has been formulated. All these assumptions, exclusions, premises, understandings, dependencies etc can collectively be referred to as caveats and should be put into a register (Figure 3.5).

figure 3.5 The Caveats Register

Serial	Caveat	Source	Resolution	Price Impact Y/N	Action

The register should be brought into being on the first day of the bid preparation and it should be the receptacle for all thoughts, ideas, concerns that are to do with the potential contract. In many instances the pre-contract risk analysis and caveats register can be merged into a single document which should be kept up to date throughout the period of bid preparation and contract negotiation.

Once contract negotiations have commenced, it may be decided to produce a version of the register for submission to the customer as a basis for structured discussions on risk allocation. This version can be suitably edited so that any concerns and tactics that are private to the company can be kept concealed and it can be appropriately modified to best suit the negotiation game plan.

As well as providing the essential function of recording all the identified caveats, the greatest purpose of the register is to keep each caveat 'open' until something positive has been done to resolve it. In principle there are only seven possible resolutions:

1) OBE – Overtaken by Events because ....
2) Risk carried by customer – expressly by contract clause ....
3) Risk carried by customer – impliedly because ....
4) Risk carried by company – expressly by contract clause ....
5) Risk carried by company – impliedly because ....
6) Company risk but covered by insurance – see policy clause ....
7) Company risk but conveyed to third party – see subcontract clause ....

In particular, categories 4 and 5 force the company to keep in mind pricing for risk. Categories 6 and 7 force the person negotiating the contract to be mindful of and interactive with other business functions such as insurance management and purchasing.

9. An effective contract

Having concluded negotiations the aim is to sign the contract as soon as possible. This aim conveys two concepts. Firstly, that the contract must be signed by two people (one from each party) and secondly, that if signature is required then the contract must be in writing. Apart from so-called speciality contracts (which cover a very small range of types of contract), there is no requirement either for signatures or for the contract to be in writing. However, written, signed contracts serve to eliminate the risk of uncertainty, both as to the intent of the parties to make their contract and as to the detail if later a question of understanding or interpretation were to arise.

Both parties will want their contract to be effective and there are four main risks to achieving this:

1) Improper formation.
2) Uncertainty.
3) Mistake.
4) Frustration.

To be properly formed a contract must satisfy the legal requirements of valuable consideration, offer and acceptance, mutual intent to create legal relations, capacity of the parties to make contracts, legality and possibility. In business contracts the only one of these that usually gives a problem is offer and acceptance. Although Lord Denning made attempts to soften the rule, the law still demands a clear offer met with an unequivocal acceptance for a contract to have been formed. The Battle of the Forms, where the parties proceed with the 'contract' without achieving a clear instant of unequivocal acceptance but 'exchange blows' in passing paperwork – quotation, purchase order, delivery note, etc – in which seller and buyer each in turn refers to his own standard contract conditions, is one example where a complete offer and acceptance can be difficult to determine. Another area of difficulty is where one side 'accepts' the other's offer 'subject to the following ...' This, strictly speaking, is a counter offer and no contract is created, and yet the parties proceed as though there were a contract. This introduces uncertainty, particularly if in the example just given the offerer then responds by commenting upon the other side's comments. This process can go on through the life of the 'contract'. If the uncertainty is to be avoided the parties must strive at the outset to ensure that there is an entire agreement reflecting a genuine offer and acceptance.

Another facet of the problem of offer and acceptance is the method of acceptance. The general rule is that acceptance must be communicated, but with the exception of acceptance under the 'postal rule' which allows acceptance to have occurred when a communication of acceptance is put into the post, whether or not the other side ever actually receives the communication. Even today cases come before the courts on the question of the postal rule. To avoid this problem the offerer should include in his offer an explicit, written statement that a contract has only come into being upon his receiving a written, unequivocal acceptance from the other side.

The word 'uncertainty' has already been used here in the sense of an entire understanding as to terms not being achieved. This would not necessarily affect the existence of the contract, only that in the extreme a court would have to imply 'missing' terms or to arbitrate between conflicting terms (but only in so far as the original intent of the parties can be deduced by the court). However, if the uncertainty is so great that a court cannot find any evidence of a common understanding then the entire 'contract' can be made void for uncertainty. To avoid this risk the parties should go to great lengths to ensure that the agreement is not only complete but also clear and unambiguous.

The final possible risks to the effectiveness of the contract are 'mistake' and 'frustration'. In both cases a court could set the contract aside. A mistake in this sense is something fundamental (such as the existence of the goods) in which the parties were in error at the time the contract was made. A frustrating event is an occurrence (such as the destruction of unique goods) which happens after the contract was made, which so fundamentally alters the position as to have been entirely outside the imagination of the parties when the contract was made. Fulsome discussion, checking, examination prior to contract should remove the risk of mistake. Frustration is theoretically a risk which is impossible to prevent, since the intervention of something completely unforeseeable cannot be dealt with in advance. However, in business contracts virtually all risks can be foreseen and dealt with in the contract and contracts voided on the grounds of frustration are rare events. Incidentally, the law does not recognise that a contract can be set aside for mistake or frustration because one side made a bad bargain. If the buyer mistakenly orders the wrong thing, that is just hard luck for him. If the seller finds that he cannot complete the contract within his budget, that is just his hard luck.

All important in avoiding these risks is to properly form a contract which is complete and certain. And yet in the dynamics of the real business world a buyer may issue a 'Letter of Intent' (LOI) or an 'Instruction to Proceed' (ITP). Although an LOI may increase the confidence of the seller that the buyer is going to proceed, the seller nevertheless goes ahead at his own risk if he starts work solely on the basis of an LOI. An ITP can be more useful if it is so drafted to be an offer of contract, albeit that it conveys only the key terms, such as a summary of the work, time frame for performance, price (or method by which price will be agreed) and payment. If the ITP is capable of acceptance then acceptance will constitute a contract, although there is then a risk that the parties will never conclude complete terms. Certainly the risk to the buyer is that, once the seller is working against an accepted ITP, there is little incentive for the seller to agree unfavourable terms which the buyer later seeks to introduce, especially since ITPs tend to be used in cases of urgency, leaving the balance of bargaining advantage with the seller.

The last point to note is that a contract need not be effective upon signature. It is permissible to include a 'condition precedent', the non-satisfaction of which would cause the contract to fail to come into existence. The most common example is a condition which requires that the seller shall have received the buyer's advance payment before the contract shall come into effect. To start work prior to the satisfaction of a condition precedent is to proceed at the risk of loss of the cost incurred and the effort deployed being wasted if the condition is not then satisfied.

10. Throwing it all away

Somewhere between making an offer and making an effective contract is the risk ·of throwing away all the good work of the bid team and securing a lemon contract. Between bid and contract there will be a period of negotiation between bidder and customer.

The negotiation is a crucial phase that can make the difference between the contract proving to be a commercial success or disaster. The golden rule of negotiation is to follow the seven Ps:

Prior
Planning and
Preparation
Prevents
Pretty
Poor
Performance.

The importance of planning, preparation, objectives analysis, rehearsal, game planning, tactics and timing in contract negotiation cannot be over-stressed. The risk of being out-smarted by the customer's ace negotiator is a real one. The company should field its strongest negotiator or negotiation team, comprised of those who have the best balance of negotiation skills, job knowledge and 'acceptability' to the customer (Figure 3.6).

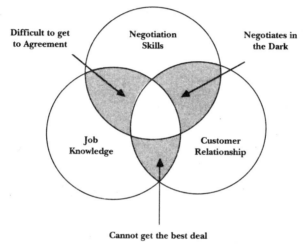

11 Contract launch

The final risk of the pre-contract stage is that those people to whom responsibility falls for the performance of the contract may not fully understand the nature of the contract, its risks and the evolution of terms through the process of contract negotiation.

The best way to mitigate this risk is to hold a contract launch meeting with the company immediately following contract award and prior to commencing the work.

Indeed, ISO9000 proposes such a review and provides a basic

*For a full analysis of the skills and risks in contract negotiation, readers are invited to refer to *Successful Contract Negotiation* by the same author, published by Hawksmere.

agenda for that purpose. All of the relevant business functions must be *required* to attend, including those not closely involved in the work.

For example, it is important for functions such as Finance (who provide project, cost and management accounting) and Personnel (who may have to recruit staff for the contract) to be as involved as those actually undertaking the project. The principal aims of the contract launch meeting are to:

1) Describe the nature, scope and time frame of the contract.
2) Identify the key terms and their meaning.
3) Review the entire pre-contract risk analysis/caveats register and explain how all the risks were dealt with.
4) Summarise the progress of the negotiations with the customer highlighting any sensitive areas to be avoided in future contract with him.
5) Identify key subcontractors, suppliers and partners and describe how dealings with them should be conducted.
6) Launch the contract risk register base on mitigating all risks residing with the company.
7) Identify the budget and cost allocations available to spending departments within the contract price.

The meeting should be properly minuted with key actions identified. In fact, ISO9000 requires a written record to be kept, but the individuals responsible for conducting the meeting must ensure that the record produced is a useful basis for undertaking the work and not a blank record produced solely for the purpose of satisfying the ISO.

2 Major sources of risk

The first three chapters have looked at the concepts and processes of commercial risk management. Succeeding chapters will take the five main sources (financial, technical, time frame, supplier and post-delivery) of risk and examine their commercial dimension, providing both an assessment of the principles and an analysis of the 'dos and don'ts'.

chapter 4

Financial risk

1 Sources of financial risk

The operation of any commercial company is one huge financial risk, made up of a vast collection of individual risks, some of which go to the heart of the particular project and some of which are relatively remote:

Near Risks	:	Is the project understood (scope and definition)?
	:	Do the designs/products exist?
	:	Are the costs accurately estimated?
	:	Are the costing/pricing rates and factors stable?
	:	Do adequate resources and capacity exist?
	:	Can reliable suppliers be found?
	:	Is the customer trustworthy?
	:	Are the contract terms understood?

Remote Risks	:	Company stability
	:	Backing of investors
	:	Strong customer base
	:	Strong product base
	:	Strong marketing activity
	:	Stable/growing market
	:	Sustainable competitive advantage
	:	Good product differentiation
	:	Stable national economy

Some of these near and remote risks may not seem like financial ·risks at all, but they are. The near risks all influence the question 'can we complete the project at a profit?' The remote risks all influence the question 'can we complete the project at a profit?' Strangely, these two questions are the same! Just as failure to understand the contract can result in real project risks not having been covered in the price, so the deterioration of the product base or marketing activity can affect the costs of the project. Certain implicit assumptions will have been made about these remote risks at the time the project was bid. That is, for example, the overheads to be recovered as part of the project assumed a certain company turnover and product margins generating overhead recovery at a certain rate. If business volume falls while the project is under way, a higher overhead burden falls to the project, adversely affecting its margin.

So whether a question surrounds a near risk (eg can we find a cheaper supplier of widgets?) or a remote risk (eg will next year's sales be on budget to generate the required private venture investment for product upgrades?) it is clear that the most volatile issue is whether the project costs can be contained within the approved estimates.

Sharing cost risk

The bearing or sharing of cost risk depends on the nature of the pricing regime for the contract:

Firm Price	:	A price which is not variable for any reason (other than change in specification, quantity or time for performance)
Fixed Price	:	A price, the final value of which is fixed by reference to some variable parameter such as an inflation index or currency exchange rate
Cost Incentive	:	A price based on the supplier's actual costs, but with buyer and seller sharing

overspends or underspends against a
pre-agreed target cost

Cost Reimbursement :   A price based on the supplier's actual
costs, plus a pre-determined amount or
percentage by way of profit

The fixed price approach deals with one or two risks only, such as
inflation and foreign currencies, both of which are dealt with later
in this chapter. The primary choice is between firm price and cost-
reimbursement which sit at opposite ends of the cost–risk spectrum
(Figure 4.1).

figure 4.1   **Cost–Risk Spectrum**

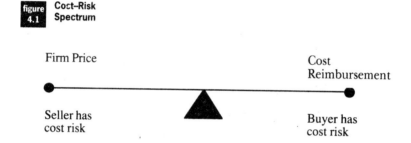

The cost incentive contract (Figure 4.2) provides the

In a conventional arm's-length relationship the seller will prefer
a firm price where he perceives the risk to be small and the
opportunity for profit great. Where the risk is high, he will prefer
cost reimbursement and hope that the buyer will have plenty of
money to cover the inevitable expenditure that will be incurred
purely as a result of the uncertainty in the contract.

The buyer's perspective is the exact opposite. The greater the
risk the more he will want a firm price arrangement so as to contain
the risk, allocate it to the other party and avoid any financial liability
beyond paying the contract price.

The cost incentive contract (Figure 4.2) provides the
compromise solution for high risk work, where neither side is willing
or able to carry the entire cost risk.

The essential principles of the cost incentive scheme are:

a) The price is agreed after the contract is completed on the
basis of costs incurred but according to a cost incentive
scheme agreed at the outset.

b) The parties agree a target cost and a cost incentive range within which the actual costs are expected to fall.

c) The parties agree a target fee which is the profit to be paid if the actual costs exactly equal the target cost.

d) The parties agree ratios in which they will share underspends or overspends against the target cost.

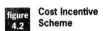

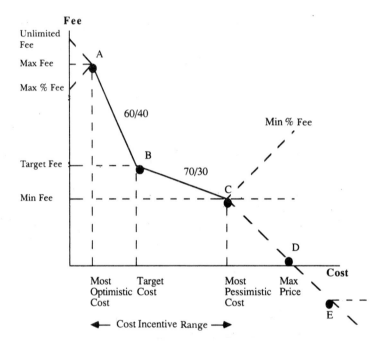

Figure 4.2 Cost Incentive Scheme

Thus the final price for the contract is the actual costs incurred, plus the target fee, plus the agreed share of savings against the target, or less the agreed share of overspends against the target.

A key difference, therefore, between a firm price and a cost incentive scheme is the tolerance within which the costs are reasonably expected to fall. For a firm price where the technical content of the contract is well understood, the cost estimating accuracy may be ±5 per cent. In a cost incentive scheme where the technical risk is much higher the tolerance around the target cost may be ±15 per cent.

Figure 4.2 is a graphical representation of a cost incentive scheme in which

Target Cost	=	Reasonable estimate assuming normal efficiency and typical problems.
Most Optimistic Cost	=	Improved efficiency and no problems.
Most Pessimistic Cost	=	Degraded efficiency resulting from and together with major problems.
Target Fee	=	Normally a percentage of the target cost.
Under-run share ratio	=	In Figure 4.2 shown as 60/40 but the ratio is negotiable.
Over-run share ratio	=	In Figure 4.2 shown as 70/30 but the ratio is negotiable.

If life were as simple as assuming that the actual costs will definitely fall within the cost incentive range, then the scheme and the graph would only run from point A to point C. However, the parties must legislate for the possibility of costs emerging outside of the two extremes where they have a number of choices:

Point A : The scheme might permit the company to continue to improve its fee at the same under-run share ratio if costs are lower than the most optimistic cost. This results in an unlimited fee opportunity. Alternatively, the parties may agree to limit the fee either in absolute or percentage terms.

Point C : The scheme might allow that for costs exceeding the most pessimistic cost the company should suffer no further erosion of its fee and a minimum fee in absolute or percentage terms should apply. On the other hand, the buyer may demand an absolute limit on its liability and include a maximum price (point D).

Point E: If a maximum price is operative, point E does not exist as the company's fee erodes at the rate of 100 per cent from point C until it reached point D, after which losses would accumulate at the rate of 100 per cent. However, in such event the buyer may agree to limit the company's liability for loss and introduce a point E, at which the curve changes shape to fix the loss in absolute or percentage terms.

This one graph shows the endless variations that can be negotiated, not only beyond the normal boundary conditions at A and C, but also between them in terms of the share ratios, target fee and cost incentive range. The great advantage of such schemes is that they are so flexible and can be tailor-made to individual circumstances, buyers and sellers.

The second great advantage of cost incentive schemes is that they promote cooperation, openness and sensible decision making between buyer and seller. If both sides are set to benefit by technical decision making and problem solving which minimises cost, then so much the better than in a firm price arrangement where the buyer is motivated to squeeze the last ounce of performance from the seller, regardless of cost to the seller.

In summary, the seller has two choices. He can pick away at individual risks (for which the succeeding do's and don'ts provide advice), or he can share the entire cost risk with his customer. The choice will depend on circumstances. Cost incentive contracts are not a panacea for all situations, but they should certainly be considered as an option in any large scale, high risk enterprise.

The Do's and Don'ts of Financial Risk

RISK – THE CUSTOMER WILL NOT PAY.

Do

a) Make payment 'of the essence of the contract'.
b) Retain title to the goods until payment is made.
c) Break contract performance into several separable parts.
d) Seek advance payments.
e) Seek milestone or stage payments.
f) Include a right to claim interest charges on overdue payments.
g) Require payments to be made under a confirmed irrevocable letter of credit.
h) Include the right to suspend work if payments are delayed.
i) Specify precisely procedure and paperwork required for invoicing.
j) Specify a maximum credit period.
k) Include a 'set off' right.

Don't

a) Use unconfirmed or revocable letters of credit.
b) Accept payment retentions.
c) Accept rolling retentions.
d) Agree to 'pay-when-paid' clauses.
e) Agree to customer 'discretion' in the making of payments.
f) Agree to vesting clauses.

In essence, when the contract is fully performed, the buyer is obliged to make payment of the contract price. From the seller's perspective reliance on this simple premise has three main drawbacks:

a) Negative cash flow while the contract is in hand.
b) No time limit on when the buyer should pay.
c) Inadequate remedies if payment is late.

Taking these in turn it is clearly the case that carrying the burden of funding work in progress under the contract is a risk. If no payment is to be made at all until the work is finished there is, at the minimum, the cost of funding the work in progress and, at the worst, there is the risk of the company becoming insolvent as no cash comes in to offset the outpouring of cash into salaries, wages, overheads, materials and suppliers. Against the buyer's wish to pay nothing until the contract is fully performed is the seller's wish to have 100 per cent of the contract price paid as an irrevocable down payment placed with order. Somewhere there is an acceptable medium between the two based on:

Advance payment	:	A proportion of the contract price placed with order.
Stage payments	:	Discrete sums of money paid as and when proportions of the work are completed.
Milestone payments	:	Discrete sums of money paid as and when specific, key tasks are completed.
Progress payment	:	Regular reimbursements of costs incurred by the seller.

The details of these arrangements should all be worked out pre-contract. Inevitably these approaches will feature in the price negotiation as the effect of them is to move the cash flow risk between buyer and seller. Having agreed to make payments while the work is in hand the protection or security that the buyer seeks is to make payments only at his discretion (ie if he is happy that good progress is being made), to achieve early passage of title in parts and materials under 'vesting', to make the payments recoverable in the event of delay or default, and to retain a sizeable element of the price until the contract is fully performed and all of the liabilities (eg including those under warranty) of the seller have been discharged. All of these are undesirable to the seller as they mean that the timing of such payments and their absoluteness are both at risk.

Unless the contract specifies the time within which valid invoices shall be paid, the seller has to fall back on the Sale of Goods Act which merely requires the buyer to pay within a reasonable time. This is too vague and open to interpretation and argument. The contract must be crystal clear that once the relevant event (eg completion of a milestone, the making of a delivery) has occurred, the seller is entitled to raise an invoice which must be settled within a fixed and specified number of days. Buyer discretion or the buyer's right not to pay until he has received monies from his customer (the 'pay when paid' regime), introduce uncertainty and therefore risk to the seller, both of which were supposed to have been avoided by the inclusion of a firm payments arrangement. Payment against a letter of credit, whereby a third party (normally a national bank in the country of the seller) will automatically pay against the proper presentation of documents defined in the contract removes this uncertainty and risk, although such arrangements are usually reserved for trading with overseas customers who may be considered of low credit worthiness, not motivated to pay and remote from effective legal action.

Finally, the seller's remedy for late payment is generally not strong. The law makes no immediate commercial linkage between performance and payment. It takes a clinical view that once the parties have exchanged their promises and made their contract the buyer is entitled to expect performance and the seller is entitled to receive payment, in that order. That is to say if 100 per cent performance is met by non-payment the seller is entitled to sue for payment and that is all. It leaves the seller with no bargaining power and no recourse other than the pursuit of his money through litigation. This principle may satisfy the lawyers, but if in the meantime the seller has gone broke, the legal principle is of little comfort to him. However, national authorities and the EC Commission have been concerned about this risk with regard to small firms in particular and the 1992 Finance Act required Government Purchasing Departments to include in contracts with their contractors terms to ensure that those contractors paid their suppliers within thirty days. Nevertheless, the prudent supplier will seek stronger contractual remedies which include a right to terminate or suspend the contract if payment is late by making payment a fundamental condition (emphasised by the words 'of the essence') of the contract. In many cases termination might injure the seller more than the buyer and as such it would be a measure of last resort. The right to retain title in the goods (so called Romalpa clauses), until full payment, can also be a powerful position in which to be since it allows the seller to recover the goods and sell them elsewhere. Again, this can be a two-edged sword since recovering the goods can be difficult, costly and unrewarding. The right to interest on late payments can be more persuasive as it is more immediate and hits the buyer where it hurts – in the pocket. In the absence of a contractual provision, recovery of 'lost interest' is not a financial loss which the courts normally recognise.

Finally, it can be as well to include a contractual right to set off in the circumstances where the buyer both buys from and sells to the seller. Thus if the buyer owes the seller money the seller can set the debt off against amounts which he owes to the buyer under a different transaction.

RISK – THE CUSTOMER CANNOT PAY.

Do
a) Investigate the financial standing of the customer pre-contract.
b) Seek bonds or guarantees from the customer's parent company (if appropriate) or from a third party such as a bank.
c) Seek credit insurance from ECGD or NCM depending on territory and status of customer.
d) Seek payment in Sterling.

Don't

a) Accept open credit terms from shaky customers.

From the seller's perspective the difference between the buyer being unable to pay and his not paying for some other reason may be largely academic. If money is owed it must be pursued although the cost of pursuit should be weighed against the value of the debt. Small debts may be better written off. Of course if the buyer has no money then pursuit of the debt is less likely to be rewarded than if the buyer simply is not paying for his own cash flow motives or as a result of a technicality. Either way the aim is to reduce or eliminate the risk of non-payment by a combination of tough contractual terms which motivate the buyer to pay (eg the right to interest on late payments), a watertight mechanism (eg the letter of credit) and the passing or sharing of the risk with an insurer (eg ECGD).

RISK – INFLATION INCREASES COST.

Do

a) Pass the risk to the buyer.
b) Seek firm (non-variable) prices from suppliers.
c) Seek long quotation validities from suppliers.

Don't

a) Assume that government inflation figures and forecasts are representative.
b) Assume that inflation rates are stable.

It is important to be precise about the term 'inflation' which is generally taken to mean the effect on costs brought about by changes in economic conditions, where economic conditions mean those generally prevailing as opposed to those specific to the company. As was seen in Chapter 5, estimating future costs when bidding for a contract must take into account, for example, the company's projected overhead rates. In some companies overhead rates are a very high element of cost which can fluctuate greatly as order book and sales wax and wane. Such local fluctuations are effectively smoothed out when absorbed into national figures. Nevertheless, passing some of the inflation risk to the buyer can be worthwhile using contract clauses variously described as 'Variation of

Price' (VOP) or 'Contract Price Adjustment' (CPA). These generally work on the basis of a formula:

$$Pa = Po \times (A + B \frac{Lf}{Lo} + C \frac{Mf}{Mo})$$

Where:

Pa	=	Contract price as adjusted
Po	=	Original contract price
A	=	Non-variable element of price
B	=	Labour proportion of variable element
C	=	Material proportion of variable element
Lf	=	Labour index final
Lo	=	Labour index original
Mf	=	Material index final
Mo	=	Material index original

The original contract price is the contract price at a particular economics base. It may be the economics prevailing at the date of contract, the date of quotation, the date of invitation to tender or any other convenient point. The contract price as adjusted is the final value of the original price after the application of the formula, albeit that interim adjustments can be made rather than wait entirely to the end. A, B and C add up to one. For example, if their values are respectively 0.1, 0.7 and 0.2, it means 10 per cent of the contract price is not variable, 70 per cent is attributable to labour which is variable and 20 per cent to material which is also variable (the labour, material proportions of the contract being 7:2). It is important to express it in this way so that it is the entire contract price (excluding the non-variable element) which is adjusted, including overheads and profit, rather than just in respect of wages/salary/material cost changes. L and M refer to inflation indices published by Industry or the Government and selected for the relevant sector of industry. Lo and Mo are the indices as at the economics base date of Po. Lf and Mf are the value of the same indices prevailing at appropriate later dates. For example, Mf may be at the mid point of material deliveries or invoices. Lf may be at, say, three months prior to due delivery reflecting the mid point of the manufacturing cycle.

In a fixed price contract the seller would prefer A to be zero conveying all the inflation risk (to the extent that movement in the chosen indices is likely to reflect actual potential changes in the particular company) to the buyer.

VOP/CPA clauses therefore tend to cover some or all of what can be referred to as 'background' inflation over which the company can exercise little control. Material costs can be controlled by seeking long-term prices and salary/wage costs can be controlled by everything from fear of redundancy to profit sharing schemes. However, buyers are generally wary of inflation clauses which link to the sellers' actual variation in wages/salaries and materials, as there is little incentive on the seller to exercise any control.

An alternative method for passing the inflation risk to the buyer if the circumstances are appropriate is to provide annual price lists for which the delivery price will be the price prevailing at date of order or at date of invoice.

RISK – FOREIGN CURRENCY FLUCTUATES ADVERSELY.

Do
a) Buy or sell forward as appropriate.
b) Look for currency commonality.
c) Pass the risk to suppliers.
d) Mitigate the risk by exchange rate variation clauses.
e) Look for payment in multiple currencies.

Don't
a) Forget to assess the currency issue at bid preparation time.

The choice (for a UK based company) of currency in which to trade depends on the circumstances:

	UK Customer paying in £	US Customer paying in £	US Customer paying in $
UK Suppliers £	√	√	X
US Suppliers £	√	√	X
US Suppliers $	X	X	√

This example is between Sterling and US dollars. This is only an example and the framework shown suits any Sterling v overseas currency situation. However, many projects involve circumstances much more complex than that shown, especially if suppliers are chosen from a wide range of overseas territories. Considerations to bear in mind are:

a) The currency in which the end customer will pay.
b) The stability of various currencies – the greater the instability the greater the risk.
c) The availability of currency.
d) The commercial advantage of paying overseas suppliers in currencies other than their own.
e) The cost of dealings in foreign currencies.

Primarily the aim is to quantify the risk so that it can be adequately provided for in the price at the time of agreeing the contract. For example, if a UK contract paid in Sterling has a large overseas supplier content, then the suppliers should be paid in Sterling (which transfers the exchange rate risk to them) or the value of the suppliers' orders should be bought forward in the relevant currencies so that the exchange rate(s) in question have been effectively fixed at the date of contract.

Alternatively, if a UK company is selling abroad to a customer who will pay in his own currency, then the currency should be sold forward or the contract should include a formula for adjusting the price for variations in price:

$$Pa = Po \times (A \frac{ER0}{ER1} + B)$$

Where:

Pa = Price as adjusted for exchange rate variation
Po = Price at date of contract
A = Variable element
B = Fixed element
ER0 = Exchange rate at base date
ER1 = Exchange rate at date of variation

Rather like the VOP or CPA formula covered earlier in this chapter, Exchange Rate Variation formulae tend to have a fixed element and a variable element. The greater the fixed element the greater the currency risk which is left with the company. The exchange rate base date might be the date of tender or date of contract. The date of variation might be the date of delivery or invoice to the customer.

An ERV formula can protect the company against all or part of the currency risk when a customer pays in other than the company's own national currency. It works by adjusting the contract price as the contract price currency fluctuates. However, an ERV formula can also be used where the customer pays in the company's national currency but where the company has significant expenditure in a different currency. So in this case the formula works by adjusting the contract price for changes in the company's costs caused by currency fluctuations in its overseas expenditure. In the formula given above the variable element (A) would be less than one reflecting the proportion of the contract price which is attributable to the overseas expenditure. ER1 would be the exchange rate at, say, the mid point of disbursement of the foreign currency.

figure 4.3 **Currency Risk Management**

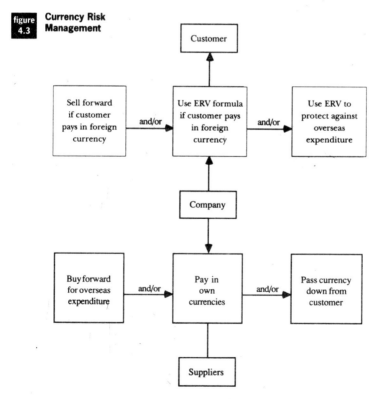

The final approach which is illustrated in Figure 4.3, together with the other currency risk management options, is having foreign currency 'flow through' the company transparently. For example, a UK customer could be invited to pay partly in Sterling and partly in the currency of the company's overseas suppliers. This completely insulates the company from the exchange rate variation risk and requires no involvement in currency dealing.

As with VOP and CPA clauses it should be remembered that ERV formulae can produce reductions in the contract price as well as increases, depending on the actual direction of movement of exchange rates.

RISK – THE CONTRACT IS TERMINATED.

Do
a) Avoid termination clauses.
b) Include the obligations on the customer to give notice of termination.
c) Include the right to recovery of costs and profits.
d) Include 'back-to-back' provisions with suppliers.

Don't
a) Assume a termination will be revoked.

Essentially a contract can come to a premature end in one of only three ways:

- By mutual agreement
- By termination for default
- By cancellation for convenience

Premature end by mutual agreement is not really a risk. A risk is something known or unknown which may or may not arise and if the risk materialises the holder of the risk has less than 100 per cent control of events.

Clearly, with that definition, termination by mutual agreement (a tautological expression if ever there was one!) cannot be a risk since neither side is bound to agree and hence total control exists.

Termination for default, whether by express contract provision or because the law allows it, is covered in detail in Chapter 6. In so far as the financial consequences are concerned the effect might be small. For example, a low value contract terminated early in its life on the basis of anticipatory breach might leave the defaulting party with little unrecoverable costs, albeit lost anticipated profits or lost business opportunity may be a bigger concern. On the other hand the impact may be very great where a large value contract is terminated for actual lateness, leaving the defaulter with huge costs, an idle workforce, unsellable part-used materials etc. However, one thing that is clear is that termination for default on a major contract is probably assessed as high impact low probability at the bid stage, thus if the risk materialises the defaulter has little control (obviously if he had control the contract would not have been late in the first place).

In a termination for default clause it is most unlikely that the innocent party will agree to compensate the defaulter in any way other than to pay for goods received and accepted. However, it is possible that a period of notice may be provided. If this obligation on the buyer to give notice can be further refined to require him to allow extra time for the seller to catch up or propose an alternative programme, so much the better.

Cancellation for Convenience is usually understood to mean cancellation for the convenience of the buyer. Rarely do contracts allow the provision to be operated vice versa. Because it is for the convenience of the buyer the buyer must accept liability for the consequences of his breaking the original deal. The frequent dilemma is over the extent of the consequences. Buyers will agree to reimburse costs properly incurred to the date of cancellation and perhaps profit on those costs but usually not anticipated profits. For these reasons it is as well for sellers to avoid cancellation for convenience clauses. A decision to take a contract may in part have been based upon anticipation of the benefits beyond making a profit on that contract. The order may take the company into a new business field or on to a grander scale of operation. For these opportunities decisions may have been made to invest in capital, acquire new premises or take on new staff. The particular order may have been taken at the expense of other more routine work. To have these opportunities and decisions potentially frustrated for no greater reason than the convenience of the buyer is wholly unattractive.

The one general exception to this view is in connection with certain types of government contract where changes in public policy may produce a justifiable reason for cancelling the contract for convenience. In the normal commercial market place, however, the most obvious situation in which the buyer would seek to cancel for convenience is where, having struck his bargain with the seller, he subsequently finds that he can get the goods cheaper or quicker elsewhere or that better products have become available. Clearly the risk that any buyer takes when he signs the contract is that he has got himself the best deal in town. In the seller's opinion the buyer should stick to the contract or, if a cancellation for convenience clause is to be included, then its terms should enshrine disincentives to the buyer to exercise the cancellation right in other than the most dire situation. The obligation to pay loss of anticipated profits or lost opportunity compensation are suitable disincentives.

Finally, it is a major risk to assume that a termination or cancellation will be revoked. Buyers may threaten one or the other in order to get the seller's attention, or as a negotiation tactic and it is important to analyse the risk of such threats being carried out (see Chapter 6). Having made such a major decision to actually cancel or terminate, it is unlikely that the buyer would revoke that decision since he, too, will have done his analysis and presumably have determined cancellation or termination to be his best possible course of action.

RISK – EXTRANEOUS FACTORS INCREASE COSTS.

Do

a) Seek contract protection for additional costs caused by
   i) Acts or omissions of the customer.
   ii) 'Force majeure' events.
   iii) Unforeseen capital requirements.
   iv) Changes in tax.
   v) Changes in the law or statutory instruments.
b) Consider liquidated damages as a financial risk limitation device.

Don't

a) Accept all embracing statements that the company carries the entire risk.

In Chapter 6 the consequences to the time frame for the project arising from the events outside the control of the company will be explored. Such events may or may not increase costs but it is as well for the contract to provide for the possibility. Extraneous events may result in additional costs as follows:

a) Investigation of resolution to the problem.
b) Introduction of extra work.
c) Original/extra work takes longer.
d) Additional effort to maintain original time frame.
e) Impact on other contracts.
f) Supplier claims echoing (a) – (e).

In the case of acts or omissions of the customer such increases can stem from:

a) Formal changes to the contract requirement.
b) Failure to approve documents, reports etc.
c) Provision of misleading advice/instruction.
d) Provision of defective material.
e) Nomination of poor suppliers.
f) Provision of inaccurate/incomplete documents, data.

The list could be quite endless and hence it is as well to have the contract provide the right of the company to increase the price, extend the time frame and modify other terms of the contract (eg payment arrangements) in respect of these acts or omissions of the buyer. Without a contractual provision, making and sustaining such claims is considerably more difficult.

Force majeure or excusable delay clauses usually protect the company only against the risk of the contract being terminated for late performance. This is very good protection but it does not compensate the company for additional cost arising from force majeure events. However, there is no legal debarment to such a principle and thus the company should seek this facility to increase the price (and to modify other affected terms) as well as extend the time frame.

Many projects require capital investment which should be identified at the bidding stage of course and as such be no concern of the buyer's per se. Sometimes the buyer wishes to approve capital expenditure and gain ownership or control of the resulting assets (eg plant, special tooling, test equipment). In this event there can be an opportunity to build into the contract a liability upon the buyer to pick up the financial consequences of acquiring capital assets additional to, or different from, those contemplated at the bid stage. This issue is a good example of how the negotiation of a contractual clause (which in this case surrounds in essence the ownership, control and disposal of capital assets) can be used as vehicle to identify and allocate liability and hence risk.

Changes in tax law that arise during the course of contract can be a major headache. One side or the other must carry this risk. The most obvious example is Value Added Tax (VAT). The difference in effect between two apparently similar contract clauses can be fundamental as regards risk bearing:

'The contract price is inclusive of VAT'

or **'The contract price is inclusive of VAT at 17.5 per cent, which will be adjusted at the date of invoice in accordance with the then prevailing legislation'.**

In the former case the risk would lie entirely with the seller, in the latter the risk is transferred to the buyer. Again this is a good example of where the choice of one form of words or another has the startling effect of moving important risks around. The 'in-between' wording of 'the contract price includes VAT at 17.5 per cent' is in itself a risk, because the buyer would interpret the reference to 17.5 per cent as information only (for VAT accounting for example) and the seller would interpret it as conveying an intent to modify the rate later if necessary. In the extreme a court would have to decide which interpretation is correct, based on custom in the trade, prior dealings and relevant correspondence (eg a price quotation).

VAT is just one tax that affects business costs. Import duty, which can be waived for certain types of contract providing certain procedures are followed and that the contract allows for it, is another example. In the ideal world the seller should pass to the buyer risk in all tax changes that affect the cost of his doing business.

Similarly, changes in other aspects of the law can cause a business to suffer increased costs (hardly ever the reverse of course). The ever tightening grip of legislation on product liability matters, the introduction of legislation on environmental issues (eg the Montreal

Protocol) and the 'minimum wage' debate under the Maastricht Social Chapter are all examples of events outside the control of companies that lead to rising costs.

The risk of rising costs in this arena can be allocated to the seller by leaving the contract silent on such matters, or to the buyer by including express terms to allow for the contract price, delivery and other terms to be varied as the events arise. Where a contract runs into delay the seller is liable to the buyer for the buyer's reasonably foreseeable financial damages resulting from delay. These are open-ended unless the contract provides an overall limit of liability of the seller, or unless delay damages are pre-estimated and fixed by the parties in a liquidated damages clause. Chapter 6 will examine liquidated damages, but in terms of management of financial risk it should be remembered that liquidated damages are a means of limiting liability rather than appearing, as they frequently do, as a form of simple penalty.

The concluding word of advice is to avoid statements or declarations in the contract that the company carries the entire risk in the performance of the work. The contract is the document that identifies and allocates the risks and such a declaration would be in conflict with this principle.

RISK – FINANCIAL CLAIMS AGAINST THE COMPANY.

Do
a) Rebut any claim received.
b) Consider making a counterclaim.
c) Muster all the defences.
d) Take legal advice.
e) Consider a financial provision.
f) Delay.
g) Blame someone else.
h) Include an overall limit of liability.

Don't
a) Admit a claim.
b) Make a financial settlement other than as a last resort.
c) Admit liability in any settlement.

Claims against the company must always be taken seriously. The sources of claims can be as follows:

Basis	Examples
■ Contractual	■ Liquidated damages
	■ Price reduction for under-performance
	■ Damages following termination
	■ Express warranties
■ Statutory	■ Implied undertakings eg under Sale of Goods Act
	■ Product safety under Consumer Protection Act
■ Legal	■ Failure in duty of care
	■ Failure against implied terms

It is important never to just admit a claim. Once admitted, liability is not in question, just the number of pound notes to make the claimant go away. Even recognising that a 'claim' has been received could prejudice the position. It is better to rebut statements made in 'your letter'. Often if a claim is made it causes the claimee to examine all the background facts, information and evidence in order to establish all possible defences, but in addition it causes him to think about the performance and behaviour of the other side. This, surprise surprise, can lead him to make a counterclaim (usually bigger!) against the claimant. If nothing else, this can be a useful bargaining card.

Whilst the vast majority of commercial claims are settled by the parties, legal advice should be sought wherever there is the possibility of the matter becoming formal, whether under conciliation, mediation, arbitration or litigation. Not only does this help to identify defences against the claim and lines of argument in commercial negotiations, but it also helps to stop the claimee from saying or doing something which might later count against it in a formal forum.

If there is any chance of money changing hands in order to resolve the claim, then a financial provision should be made in the company's books of account so that the risk of having to part with cash is planned into the business model. If this heart-rending act of the company parting with its money appears inevitable, then the longer it takes the better. After all, if the delay is long enough the claimant may give up. The possibility of blaming (ie transferring the liability for the risk that has materialised) someone else should always be considered. This has two avenues. Firstly as a bluff which, if it works, is fine. Secondly, and going back to first principles, the contract may allocate the particular risk to the other party despite what common sense may indicate to the contrary.

If a deal has to be done it should always be without admission of liability and without prejudice and, if possible, without hard cash. Parties who trade with each other beyond a single transaction may well have things to offer other than cash. A discount on the next contract, dropping of another separate claim, are examples of cash free settlements.

The final financial risk management device the company should consider is the inclusion in the contract with his customer of an overall limit of liability. Some liabilities (eg for personal injury or death) cannot be excluded, some liabilities can be limited (eg property damage limited to the value of insurance), some liabilities can be transferred (eg to complete on time if prevented by force majeure) but ultimately the company is liable to the customer for the performance of the contract and to some lesser or greater extent for the consequences of failure in some respect or another. With the exception of liabilities such as those just mentioned, such a contract is said to be an 'unlimited liability contract'. To identify all the possible liabilities and fix a limit for each one in negotiation is impracticable. And yet the carrying of unlimited liability contracts is the very worst of financial risks that a company can take. There have been examples where a major, successful company has been destroyed by just one unlimited liability contract going wrong, bringing down financial liabilities which either had not been foreseen and hence had not been provided for, or which were too huge once they had materialised for the company to cope with.

The solution is to include in the contract a limit of liability (ie limiting the seller's liability to the buyer) in respect of the entire contract. Properly worded (care is required because clauses excluding or limiting liability are not always popular with the courts – see Chapter 1) the company's liability to the buyer would then be limited to, say, the value of the contract or perhaps a small number of multiples thereof. Buyers should accept this sort of limitation provided the limit is not too low and having a limit is good risk management for the company. However, such clauses do not limit the liability of the seller to third parties for which other measures are necessary – see Chapter 8.

5

Technical risk

1 Do we want to take this risk at all?

Business is about taking risks. Take a contract and you take a risk. The risk is that you may not be able to complete the work on time and within budget. Cost and time are the key issues and in all but the simplest contracts the scale and complexity of the technical requirements of the contract are the main driving forces on cost and time. If the technical scale and complexity are not understood then cost will increase and the work will take longer. The cost will increase not only because there is more work to do than had been realised but also because more work usually takes longer. More time almost always means more money.

Bidding for contracts of high complexity and long duration inevitably invites the question as to whether taking the risk on at all is a wise move. In a difficult economic environment any business is good business. The company that consistently chooses not to bid because the risks are too high has no work and no future. Its fate is sealed and it may as well issue the redundancy notices straightaway. However, the company that bids and wins high risk work which it does not fully understand is only delaying its fate. Contracts which overrun on time or underachieve on performances tend to lead to customer dissatisfaction. Contracts which overrun on budget tend to disillusion shareholders. The combination of dissatisfied customers and disillusioned shareholders is not the best recipe for long-term business survival!

And yet not bidding for work which is obviously in the company's market sector and ostensibly within its capability and capacity is not a serious option. The answer to the question 'do we want to take this risk?' is 'No, but we will'. Unless the company is able to diversify into lower risk markets where there is market share to be won against the sitting suppliers, then inevitably the conclusion must be drawn that bidding is the only choice. The objectives then become to understand properly the scale and complexity of the requirement and find ways of reducing, eliminating or sharing the risk inherent in the potential contract.

Analysing the requirement

The twin problems of bidding high complexity contracts are not enough time and not enough money. And yet in the bid phase there are assumptions and decisions made which will forever affect the performance of the contract. It is far better to bid fewer jobs, having spent as much effort as possible understanding the requirement, than to bid as many as possible hoping it will be all right on the night.

For a complex requirement spread over a number of years the risks that can have an impact include:

a) Rate and direction of technology evolution.
b) Rate and direction of manufacturing process evolution.
c) Availability of IT support (eg CAD/CAM).
d) Evolution of new software languages, tools and development environments.
e) Obsolescence of designs, materials and components.
f) Scale and complexity underestimated.
g) Changing technology in the customer environment.
h) New or revised statutory requirements on standards, procedures, inspection and health and safety matters.

All risks of this type should appear in the programme risk analysis and also in the commercial risk analysis if there are issues which are not purely technical eg the performance to specification of key suppliers.

3 Options

One approach in handling these sorts of matters is to offer the customer options that allow a low risk path to meeting his entire requirement. If the technical requirement contains, for example, 10,000 features which have to be met and the pre-contract programme risk analysis shows only a 5 per cent probability of delivering all 10,000 features on time, then it can be much better to offer initial delivery with limited functionality followed by phased upgrades over time which represent a growing capability culminating in total performance. This approach is lower risk to both sides. The company carries a lesser risk of encountering contractual and cost penalties and of running into trouble. The customer enjoys a greater probability of receiving 'something that works' on time with a reliable path towards full specification.

4 Sharing the risk

The ultimate logic for the customer to consider is that leaving all risk in the performance of the contract with the company does not equate to eliminating the risk of the contract being performed on time and to specification. Hence, if there is significant risk in the work, it can be more prudent to accept that managing the risk is best a joint activity. After all, even if contractually all risk lies with the company, this can in practice be of little consolation to the customer if the contract is delivered late or at under performance.

The best means of sharing the technical risk is to share the cost-risk. Technical uncertainty means uncertainty over cost. Hence if technical decisions are made jointly in an environment where both sides together stand to gain or lose financially, depending upon the quality of those decisions, then the greater the incentive for sound decision making. The principles of cost-risk were discussed in Chapter 4. At the heart of the concept is the idea that if the company turns in efficient performance and enjoys a fair wind, then its rate of profit increases while at the same time the cost of the job to the customer falls. If the work turns out to be more problematic than anticipated and the company is unable to produce optimum efficiency, then profit is eroded and cost to the customer increases. This principle can operate perfectly well in a contract where the company remains fully responsible for entire performance and yet the idea of technical risk sharing seems to disturb the normal, clinical contractual regime. The point is that, on the face of it, the customer's normal ability to hold the company liable for the consequences of poor or late performance may be compromised if the customer participates in decision making or otherwise directs the work. While the prudent customer will be aware of this risk and, indeed, while the shrewd company will be aware of this 'opportunity', the practice of it is that jointly considered problems usually produce better answers and the risk of jeopardy to the customer's position need not be great. In fact the company may agree to the contract denying that joint decisions waive the customer's rights as the benefit of that approach significantly reduces the risk of poor or late performance.

Furthermore, the cost risk sharing scheme can be modified actually to allow variation in the achievement against the technical requirement (Figure 5.1).

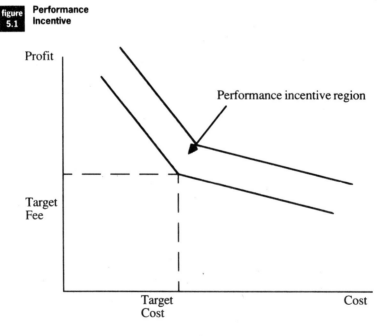

figure 5.1 Performance Incentive

In a scheme such as this, additional profit can be earned from bettering specified minimum standards of technical achievement, providing both the opportunity for improved profits through pure cost management and additionally through a specific performance related formula.

5. The commercial engineer

Many large contracts and projects absolutely rely upon 'engineers' to undertake or participate in crucial activities such as:

a) Estimating costs.
b) Estimating time.
c) Producing outline designs, prototypes at the tender stage.
d) Producing complex designs, products and systems in contract.
e) Producing technical proposals as part of the bid.
f) Producing 'implementation' specifications in response to 'requirement specifications'.
g) Producing specifications and statements of work for subcontractor/supplier request for quotation.
h) Project manage the contract.
i) Generate change proposals.
j) Handle the day-to-day interface with customers and suppliers.

The importance of ensuring that the engineers who bear the responsibility for those activities are commercially aware as well as professionally competent cannot be overstated. The legal, contractual and financial implications of their actions should be an essential part of their understanding of their responsibilities. It is as easy to lose £100,000 on a £250,000 contract as it is to lose it on a £24,000,000 contract. The development of 'commercial engineers' should be seen as a strong plank in the overall process of commercial risk management. The elimination or management of risks once the contract is under way relies upon the calibre and knowledge of the flesh and blood people involved. If those personnel charged with the successful performance of the contract are not aware of all the risks, then risk management can at best be a half-baked affair.

6. The do's and don'ts of technical risk

RISK – THE REQUIREMENT IS ILL-DEFINED.

Do
a) Ensure that specifications are included in the contract.
b) Include a statement of precedence.
c) Include a compliancy statement.
d) Adopt the minimum interpretation of the requirement.
e) Consider the commercial implications when ambiguities are resolved.
f) Keep a proper record of decisions made or directions given by the customer.

Don't
a) Agree that the customer is always right!

The key symptom of poorly defined technical requirements is 'requirement creep'. This is the process by which the gulf between the company's subconscious minimal expectation of the work required and the customer's subconscious excessive expectation materialises and widens. Technical requirements can often be ill-defined because lack of time, thought or foresight by the customer in drafting the request for quotation, or by the company in responding, mean that neither party is clear in its own mind as to exactly what the contract requires and certainly mutual understanding, which is the cornerstone of every good contract, is absent from the equation. Nevertheless, the initial simple measure to avoid this problem is to ensure that there is at least a specification in the contract. In this context the word specification is just used to mean some detailed statement of the technical requirements. If the contract includes a specification then this must be better than some general statement. However, it is necessary to consider this in a little more depth. Using the word specification in this generic sense, then the possibilities include:

Drawings
Manufacture	–	Engineering drawings which show what to make.
Process	–	Information which shows *how* to make.

Specifications

Performance	–	A definition of what the product does.
Technical	–	A definition of what the product is.
Acceptance	–	A definition of the method of proof of compliance.
Statement of Work	–	A qualitative description of the activities involved.

The more such documents are included the better the definition of the requirement. However, if there is more than one document then the potential problem is introduced of mutual exclusiveness, inconsistency or ambiguity between the documents. This must be overcome by including a statement saying which document has precedence in the event of conflict. The choice of specification type can have the effect of allocating risk between one side or the other. If the customer specifies manufacturing and process drawings with which the company complies, then the risk must lie with the customer if the end product does not meet his needs.

Similarly, if the customer contracts against a performance specification, then the risk of failure must lie with the company. The inclusion of a statement of work (SOW) can both help and hinder the situation. A SOW can confuse the position if full compliance with the technical specification requires additional work to that stated in the SOW. Who then carries the liability for the cost of the extra work? On the other hand, the SOW may indeed help in the understanding of what is to be done and so may have a place in the scheme of things. If an acceptance specification is used to define the method of proof of compliance then the status of individual requirements of the technical specification which are not explicitly to be proven (for cost or practicality reasons) under the acceptance specification must be made clear.

So clarity can be improved by incorporating appropriate specifications in the contract and by stating an order of precedence in the event of conflict between them. Further clarity can be gained by including a compliancy statement which, for example, lists every paragraph of each specification against which is put a statement of compliance. This can be a simple 'yes' or 'no' or a quantitative statement can be given for partial compliancy.

However, these steps improve clarity but may not of themselves eliminate the tendency for requirement creep. As the work proceeds and gaps or ambiguities in the requirement emerge the customer will apply pressure to the company in engineering liaison meetings or 'progress' meetings to accept that the extra work is implicitly required and should be undertaken. The desire to make progress, to keep the customer happy and perhaps to achieve payment milestones produces acquiescence on the part of the company's engineering community who are intimately involved with the customer at such meetings. To resist requirement creep personnel so involved must always put the minimum interpretation on the requirement, understand the commercial implications of going beyond what was anticipated and keep written records of meetings and other avenues through which the customer attempts to make the requirement creep. Once engineering staff understand that innocently concurring with the customer's view can lead to the contract running into a loss or being terminated (ie because the extra work cannot be completed in the contract time frame), then they pretty soon take a more commercial view of life. This may sound an obvious statement (and injurious to commercially aware engineers!) but it must be remembered that 99 per cent of most engineers' professional training is to do with 'volts, amps and ohms' and not with the harsh realities of contract law. Training engineering staff who come into contact with the outside world on these realities is a key feature of commercial risk management.

A good starting point in such training is that the customer is *not* always right, particularly when it comes to extra work not allowed for in the cost or time estimates used at the date of contract negotiation. Once this basic instinct is instilled the company's position is the better protected.

RISK – THE REQUIREMENT KEEPS CHANGING.

Do
a) Operate strict contract change control procedures.
b) Include a contractual entitlement to price revisions etc.
c) See the fluidity as an opportunity.
d) Use urgency as a bargaining tool.
e) Include 'back to back' provisions with subcontractors.

Don't
a) Implement changes prior to price agreement.

b) Ignore cash flow implications.

c) Accept unrealistic changes.

Having established a sound statement of specification (the 'technical baseline') in the contract the customer's ability to alter the specification can either arise because the contract gives him the right to vary the requirement, or if he seeks the agreement of the seller to modify the contract. The latter gives the company a much stronger bargaining position since it is not obliged to accept any variation and for this reason the customer may seek a contractual right to issue variation notices. It is important to be clear as to which parts of the contract requirement are subject to this unilateral right of variation. The right may be limited to matters of pure technical specification or may extend to quantity and time frame. In any event the contract should define strict procedures for controlling changes to the technical baseline. The procedures should require that proposals for contract change examine:

a) Effect on price (the particular contract and other related contracts).

b) Effect on performance.

c) Effect on time.

d) The date of implementation.

e) Before and after implications (eg backwards compatibility).

f) Effect on operation, maintenance, spares holdings.

The company should be clear on whether it would recommend particular changes and take responsibility for their success, or not recommend particular proposed changes and leave the risk of their success with the customer. Both sides may wish the right to propose changes with, in most cases, only the customer having the right to decide. The contract should also provide for liability for proposal preparation costs. Most importantly the contract must prescribe that the requirement changes do entitle the company to revisions to price, time for performance and adjustment of other affected features of the contract.

Contract changes, although potentially disruptive, are nevertheless an opportunity in several senses. More work means more order book and turnover. More work means price increases with a chance to improve profits in negotiation with the captive customer as compared with the profit potential at the bidding stage. More work means more time which allows at least a muddying of the water and a dilution of the original time frame obligation. Similarly, the urgency with which changes must be introduced can be a powerful bargaining tool in the process of renegotiating the price and other aspects of the contract.

The right of the customer to change the contract should be echoed in the terms of subcontracts so that changes dictated by the customer that affect subcontract work do not leave the company powerless to obey and thus in breach of contract. There is a delicate balancing act to be achieved here in so far as subcontract price revisions should not be agreed prior to equivalent revisions being negotiated to the contract price.

The main thrust of the bargaining advantage to the company is in avoiding the obligation to introduce changes prior to agreeing a price revision. To do otherwise runs the risk of negotiation being left until the contract is finished. This situation hands the bargaining advantage back to the customer who has the goods and the money! Thus the company should hold out for agreeing changes prior to going ahead. This is also important from a cash flow point of view. To proceed without prior adjustment to price and payment arrangements runs the risk of real extra cost being incurred beyond the limits of the contract payment scheme, exposing the risk of negative cash flow and financing costs.

Whilst changes are an opportunity for the company since, in the words of the customer, 'the price only ever goes up', the company should be wary of changes which reduce the scope or the scale of the contract to the point where the contract is no longer commercially attractive or of changes which are unrealistic or impossible to implement. Changes which are uneconomic of achievement or unrealistic (eg halving the time frame) are wholly undesirable and it can be as well to put lower boundary conditions on the customer's right to vary the contract.

RISK – THE WORK TAKES LONGER THAN EXPECTED.

Do
a) Follow the do's and don'ts in Chapter 6.
b) Handle the customer interface carefully.
c) Consider renegotiating the contract.

Don't
a) Give ill-considered promises.

Technical difficulty and delay are obviously inter-linked. Technical difficulty is only one reason that can cause delay. Chapter 6 looks at the risks and issues surrounding time frame but it could be argued that there is a special class of technical problem which is genuinely unpredictable. This is distinct from technical problems causing delays where the root problem is poor understanding, poor estimating or poor performance (eg under-resourcing the contract). The pure technical issue is the one where, notwithstanding prudent and professional estimating and adequate resourcing, there emerges a problem beyond the expectation of the reasonable man and therefore beyond whatever allowances were made in cost and time for contingent events. This situation must be tackled judiciously with the customer. Apart from the problems that this type of difficulty will cause the company the emergence of an unpredicted technical issue may generate loss of confidence by the customer, triggering a chain reaction that could culminate in termination.

The resolution of technical problems is inherently a part of any contract involving complex or 'high tech' work, but the emergence of that special category of problem, if it should be of a significant scale, could well be the event that brings down rack and ruin. The usual reaction of the company (beyond the normal tactics of finding someone else to blame) is to concentrate on the time factor with a view to persuading the customer that all will be well, if only a little more (and a little more, and a little more!) time could be allowed. This makes good sense in many cases but there is a risk that soldiering on can become an indefinite process with an indeterminate end. The company should very carefully examine the situation to see if this is likely to be the case and, if so, consider an early attempt to renegotiate the contract, not just to extend the time but to reduce the requirement in such a way that the issue is effectively removed. It can be better to reduce the scope and the price by 10 per cent than to overrun the price by 20 per cent in order to achieve 100 per cent of the scope.

The consequences and difficulties of renegotiating the contract should not be underestimated. The customer is not obliged to go down this path, the requirement giving rise to the technical problem may be an absolutely mandatory feature in the customer's eyes and, if to get it removed the customer wants a 30 per cent reduction in price for a 5 per cent reduction in performance, then the decision for the company is certainly not an easy one. However, the point is that renegotiation should be given early consideration, even if it is not raised with the customer until later, rather than flogging on regardless. Part of the equation will be the respective bargaining positions of the two sides and their relative negotiating strengths and weaknesses. Certainly if the approach is attempted it must be properly planned and executed with the company being sure of its ground at each step. For example, it is nothing short of foolish to confess that 'we cannot meet 100 db but we can achieve 98 db' only later to find, after the customer has accepted that 98 db will do, that only 95 db can be attained.

RISK – THE WORK NEVER FINISHES.

Do
a) Instill engineering discipline.
b) Define completion and acceptance.
c) Seek entitlement to concessions.

Don't
a) Wait for customer approval per se.

The difference between the risk 'the work never finishes' and 'the work takes longer than expected' is perhaps a little obscure. The latter covers the situation where a substantial problem occurs which may be utterly insoluble or not soluble within a cost or time frame which is remotely comparable with the contract as agreed. The risk of the work never finishing is more to do with the attitude of the people in both the customer and company organisations. Theoretical legal 'get outs' in respect of the substantial problem such as 'frustration' or 'impossibility' are difficult to establish and of little practical help in the real world. Although the customer probably has no interest in the cost penalty to the company in solving such a problem, if the contract is likely to take five years instead of the contracted one year, some major deal must be done between the two sides if the customer's overall need remains undiminished and he has no practical alternative. Contrast this with the situation where the work drags on because the company's engineers 'won't stop engineering it', or the customer's people are excessively pedantic in declaring the work complete.

Thus, if this distinction is accepted, the issue becomes one of ensuring that the engineering team is disciplined to meet the requirement and no more and that not only is the requirement defined but also that completion and acceptance are clearly described (see also Chapter 8). The other issue here is the application of Pareto's law. The final 5 per cent of the work or the last ounce of performance may soak up a degree of time and money which is hugely disproportionate to the ostensible intrinsic value or to the true worth to the customer. Notwithstanding that the last drop of performance may be entirely incidental to the real needs of the customer, he is nevertheless perfectly entitled to insist upon 100 per cent performance. Therefore it can be extremely useful for the contract to include a provision allowing concessions to be granted against the contract requirement. The really clever bit is to draft the provision so that the customer is bound to approve concessions, perhaps limited in some qualitative or quantitive way to marginal, or non-serious deficiencies only. The disadvantage is that the customer may wish an entitlement to some price reduction but concurring with such unreasonable demands may well represent the best compromise!

The other risk to achieving a tidy and timely close to the contract is the situation in which completion or acceptance requires positive action by the customer. From the company's viewpoint the contract should be so constructed that discharge of the company's obligations can be a matter of objective determination. Thus, clauses which for example specify that the company 'must work to the satisfaction of the customer' or that require the 'customer to issue an acceptance certificate' introduce an unacceptable degree of subjectivity which is both unnecessary and wholly undesirable given that the customer is under no incentive to confirm that the company has discharged its obligations.

RISK – PERFORMANCE FAILURE.

Do
a) Avoid 'turnkey' obligations.
b) Avoid performance specifications.
c) Avoid certifying 'fitness for purpose'.

Don't

a) Hold the company out as an expert.

The title of this risk is performance failure. In this sense the word performance means performance of the contract. Thus a failure of performance would in strict terms only be absolutely apparent at the due date for performance or at some stage after delivery. Thus this risk could have been left to be dealt with in Chapter 8. However, it is covered here on the basis that the essential technical obligation is fixed at the outset of the contract and the extent to which that obligation represents a risk is determined by the terms of contract. Thus if the obligation is, for argument's sake, termed the objective, then for a defined objective (ie as might be captured in a technical specification), the degree of risk to the company would depend upon the type of contract:

Type of Contract	Sentiment	Risk to the Company
Study/Research	Do the best you can	Nil
Development	Produce a design which looks as though it would meet the objective	Medium
Manufacture	Make what is described in the drawings	Medium
Turnkey	Design and make something that definitely meets the objective	High

A degree of licence has been used in drawing these sentiments but they serve to illustrate the point. The ultimate 'turnkey' contract leaves all the risk in everything (design, materials. workmanship, construction etc) with the company until the who[illegible]s proved itself complete. Such risks should be avoided and there lies the dichotomy. Going back to one of the first principles of commercial risk management, ownership of risk is in effect bought and sold between the parties. The whole purpose of the customer adopting a turnkey strategy is to leave all risk with his supplier and, indeed, a main plank in the company's selling message may be its willingness to carry and its ability to manage the risk. Thus there is the risk-opportunity balance to be considered, but that does not necessarily mean that the company should sign up for a completely open-ended contractual liability.

The other use of the word performance is in the context of a specification which says what the product must do as opposed to what it is. Performance specifications therefore imply a greater burden and risk for the company as they can be construed as taking the commitment into the post-delivery period. Similarly, contracts which require the company to certify that the goods are 'fit for purpose', introduce the possibility that proof of compliance with the contract relies on demonstrating after the event a capability which may be subjectively or vaguely described. In simple terms the company aims to leave the risk of having ordered or specified the wrong thing with the customer. The company needs to appear as a 'non intelligent' supplier selling to an 'intelligent customer'. The company should avoid holding itself out as 'an expert' or accepting that the customer has relied upon its skill and judgement as both these reinforce the liability which the customer would seek to impute to the company. Inevitably there is the trade-off between reputation, selling message etc and protection against legal and contractual risk but again, at the very least, the delicacy of this balance should be acknowledged.

RISK – CUSTOMER PROVIDED INFORMATION, MATERIAL OR FACILITIES INADEQUATE.

Do

a) Include an obligation on the customer to provide the information, material or facilities by certain dates and for certain periods.

b) Include a definition of customer-provided information, material and facilities.

c) Include a customer warranty that information, material and facilities are adequate and fit for purpose.

d) Include an entitlement to revise the contract if the customer's obligations are not honoured.

Don't

a) Assume responsibility and risk for the customer's obligations.

Where performance of the contract depends on information, material or facilities to be provided by the customer, his obligation to do so by certain dates and for certain periods should be stated in the contract.

Failure against these obligations may give rise to delay. Delay may also be caused by the dates being achieved but the information, material or facilities proving inadequate. The customer's liability for the risk of the time and cost effects of delay are covered in Chapter 6. However, it is not inconceivable that lateness or inadequacy of these things does not delay the performance of the contract but does increase its costs through nugatory and diverted effort expended prior to the realisation that, for example, the customer-provided information is inadequate or the expense incurred in having to 'work around' the problem.

For those reasons it is important to state for example that customer-provided information will be in a specified form and format and that the customer warrants that it is 'complete, up-to-date and fit for purpose'. Similarly, customer-provided material and facilities should be subject to equal rigour in definition and warranty. The contract must expressly provide the company with the entitlement to revise the price and other affected features of the contract in the event that any customer obligation is not properly discharged.

If the contract has been concluded on the basis of the customer providing information, material or facilities, then that 'sine qua non' should not be disturbed by a clause that transfers the risk in that provision to the company. For example, clauses which require the company to satisfy itself that customer provided information is fit for purpose should be avoided.

RISK – SUBCONTRACTOR WORK WILL NOT INTEGRATE.

Do
a) Use performance specifications.
b) Tie the subcontractor into the customer contract.
c) Specify acceptance testing based on the customer's contract.
d) Follow the do's and don'ts of Chapter 7.

Don't
a) Pretend to be the expert.

If avoiding performance specifications in the contract with the customer is a good idea, then using them in subcontracts must also be a good idea. If significant elements of the work are to be subcontracted, then one of the greatest risks is in defining the technical content of the subcontractor's work in such a way as to ensure that the end product will co-work or integrate with other elements, whether undertaken by the company or by other subcontractors. The situation can become very complex (Figure 5.2).

 Technical Interfaces

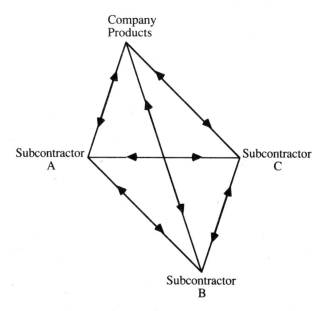

The number of technical interfaces between pairs and sets of products emanating from different sources can be manifold. If the company specifies for example an interface specification for one subcontractor to meet, then the company carries all the risk in the consequences of failure on the other side of the interface. Hence the preference for performance specifications in addition to interface specifications so as to create some obligation to the subcontractor which straddles both sides of the interface:

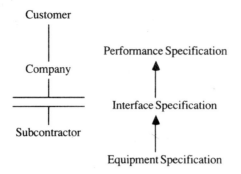

Provided the subcontractor signs up to the performance specification, which should be reflective of the end contract to some extent, then the subcontractor becomes tied into the customer contract. Similarly, acceptance of the subcontractor's work should be defined in such a way that the products are tested so as to demonstrate compliance with the relevant features of the end contract. At the heart of this issue is the question as to who is the expert. The company's engineer may feel he is the expert in the product field and certainly in so far as his responsibility is concerned for meeting the requirements of the customer's contract. He may thus feel it is his task and his alone to specify (content, scope, method) what is required of each subcontractor. While this is laudable it is also dangerous, as it may allow the subcontractor to escape from what quite reasonably should be his liability. The engineer may also feel that this part of his job is purely 'technical' and nothing at all to do with his purchasing, commercial or contract manager. This too is dangerous. Just as it is unwise for the purchasing manager to think that he does not need any help in drafting the subcontract, the engineer who sees matters as either technical or not is misguided. Whether selling or buying, the contract or subcontract should be jointly crafted so as to achieve the optimum construction that satisfies the technical need while minimising commercial risk.

chapter

6

Time frame risk

Bidding compliant delivery

The risk of not completing the contract on time arises either before contract award and/or during contract performance:

Sources of time frame risk

Pre-contract award : Requirement not fully understood
                   : Resources underestimated
                   : Elapsed time for performance underestimated
                   : Resources planned to be free do not become available

Post-contract award : Loss of key resources
                   : Work proves more difficult than expected
                   : Customer delays the work
                   : Suppliers delay the work
                   : Extraneous forces delay the work

On the one hand the key question of resources ought to be the one area in which the company can exercise the greatest control because the recruitment and deployment of resources is virtually entirely within the company's control. However, the build-up of resources for a project remains a typical problem (Figure 6.1).

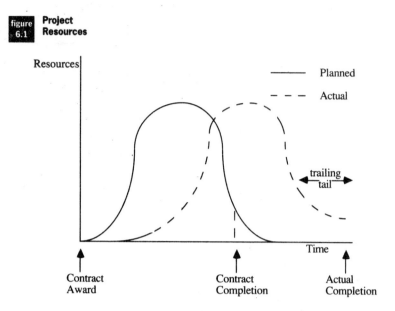

figure 6.1 **Project Resources**

This shows the typical position whereby an early, steep build-up of resources is planned, with a relatively short peak and a steady run-down as the contract is completed on time. In practice the build-up starts late and does not grow as steeply as required, leading perhaps to a higher peak and possibly a trailing tail as completing the entire contract proves more complicated and demanding than expected.

In theory these problems can be avoided. Good management of resources will prevent this resource allocation problem. Good estimating will ensure the requirements are fully understood. Good planning, project management and programme risk management will ensure that the contract is completed on time and within budget. However, life is not perfect and unexpected things do arise to interfere with contract performance. Nevertheless, the company ought to be as clear as possible at the bid stage as to the likely turn of events:

Delivery		Bid		Anticipate		
No problem	=	Compliant	+	On time	=	No worry
Problem – Option 1	=	Non-compliant	+	On time (to offered performance)	=	No worry
Problem – Option 2	=	Compliant	+	Late	=	RISK

118

So bidding compliant delivery with a high expectation of completing on time should not be a problem either in terms of bid adjudication or contract performance. Bidding non-compliant on delivery to eliminate risk of delay in contract performance is sound so that customer and company are both clear as to the position and the risk of contract penalties are avoided. However, this runs the risk that the company may be ruled out at the bid stage for non-compliance and this leads to the decision to adopt the final option which is to bid compliant having a high expectation of lateness. This approach can be said to be unethical but in the hard commercial world it can be a key tactic in securing business. The customer's own risk analysis at the bid stage may draw him to his own conclusions about the viability of individual bids on time frame matters but, at the end of the day, the company is entitled to take the view that winning the contract and then working to eliminate delay or to persuade the customer that some delay is tenable is a legitimate approach.

The time frame obligation

The seller's obligation to complete the contract by a specified date is a fundamental one. If the contract does not specify a completion date then the Sale of Goods Act comes into operation and obliges the seller to complete within a reasonable period. However, the rule implied by the Sale of Goods Act does not usually apply to commercial contracts as it is rare for a commercial contract not to indicate the required completion date in some way.

The complication is that many large contracts specify many dates on or by which things are supposed to be done and so the question must arise as to whether all such dates are equally important in so far as the fundamental obligation is concerned.

Both buyer and seller have a dichotomy to answer on this point. On the face of it the buyer wants to have it absolutely clear that he has not accepted any part of the work until the whole is complete and that the whole must be complete by no later than one specified date. On the other hand, key events or milestones along the way for which the contract mentions date can be critical to him in assessing progress of the work and perhaps in deciding to release interim payments. Thus he does not want these dates to be of secondary importance. The seller would not wish to have any dates carry great significance in case he runs into trouble and yet he would like to have the contract constructed so as to permit 'partial performance', which permits that the work can be completed and accepted in stages so that early stages once accepted by the customer are forever accepted, even if the entire contract is never completed. This construction implies that individual stages could well have specified dates, the meeting of which individually carry the weight of fundamental obligation.

To bring this sharply into focus it must be said that failure to complete on time allows the buyer the remedy of termination. Thus it must be made clear in the contract whether only the final date or milestone dates as well allow the termination remedy if it, or they, are missed. The seller must try to avoid milestone dates carrying this penalty and careful drafting of the contract can still permit partial performance and staged irrevocable acceptance by the buyer. Regardless of the status of milestone dates, if progress is patently slow or other evidence (such as progress reports by the seller) exists as to indicate the contract to be most unlikely to be performed on time, the buyer can anticipate the breach of contract and terminate immediately.

3: Of the essence

'Time is of the essence of the contract' is a statement which buyers are traditionally recommended to include in the contract and sellers are urged to avoid. The truth of the matter is that in business contracts (except those for building works) time is usually considered to be of the essence provided dates are specified, whether or not this expression is included. The effect of it is therefore only to emphasise the implied condition. To be sure of avoiding the duty to meet particular dates the contract should state that time is not of the essence. This defeats the general assumption about the nature of business contracts. It is not so peculiar as it sounds. Despite the general assumption, timeliness is not invariably important and the seller thus avoids the risk of the buyer later deciding that it is. As with most things it is important for the contract to be clear one way or the other.

4 Consequences of delay

Whilst unplanned delay is bad news for the company in terms of additional costs, delayed payments, negative cash flow and other such effects that have an impact upon its operation, potentially the biggest risk is the customer taking action beyond exercising those provisions of the contract which are aimed at 'focussing the company's attention' eg suspending payments.

The two ultimate remedies available to the buyer are termination of the contract and damages.

The law expects the contracting parties to keep to their bargain. If the seller fails to complete on time then the buyer is not expected to wait even a reasonable time. If the delay is one day or one hour or minute beyond the due time the buyer can terminate summarily for default. The buyer may want to reinforce this right by having a contract clause to the same effect. This gives the seller some opportunity to open out a debate at the time of contract regarding periods of notice or cure, but essentially the buyer will be looking for a simple contractual statement of what is his legal right.

In the event of default the buyer is entitled to recover damages from the seller to the extent necessary to compensate him for any financial loss suffered. In this context 'compensate' means recovery of loss suffered and the loss suffered is strictly financial loss. In damage of this kind there is no sense of payment to compensate for upset or injured feelings and the loss must be real and not notional.

Damages that can be recovered are those which flow directly from the default and are not those consequent upon it. There is no good definition of direct and consequential damages since the distinction is not absolute, it depends upon the particular circumstances. This is because the core principle is one of foreseeability. That is, the defaulting seller is liable for those damages suffered by the buyer which were reasonably foreseeable by the seller at the time the contract was made. Thus in the absence of the buyer having explicitly told the seller of the potential consequences of delay, the degree of foreseeability would be dependent upon the circumstances. For example, there was a case where a construction company contracted with a local electricity generating company to provide a major on-site power supply. As it turned out the power was interrupted causing the construction company to have to demolish a part-built aqueduct which was being built using a method of continuous pouring of concrete. The construction company failed in its law suit against the power company for the complete cost of demolition and rebuild of the aqueduct as the court held that the power company could not reasonably have foreseen the consequences of a break in power supply, as it could not have been expected to know of the continuous pour method employed.

The most obvious example of buyer direct damages flowing from a seller's default is the possible additional cost of purchasing elsewhere. Again, buyers' preference is to include the 'purchase in default' remedy as an express contract condition. It can be as well for the parties to decide how far the liability for damages should go and determine a list of potential categories of potential damage for inclusion in the contract. However, neither side is usually disposed towards this clinically correct approach beyond trying either totally to include or exclude everything generically consequential. Particularly for the seller, it is as well to avoid any contractual statement conveying liability for consequential damages, as he may consider it better to argue it out later if the need should ever arise.

The buyer's right to recover damages arises whether or not he elects to terminate the contract. He may choose to continue with the contract if it remains the best opportunity to acquire the goods in an acceptable time frame. In continuing with the contract he does not lose his right to damages. However, if he does continue he can lose his right to terminate. After all, it can be said to be unfair to the seller for the buyer to let him continue, thus increasing his expenditure against the possibility of termination and so a termination should be executed promptly following default. The buyer might think otherwise. He may consider it both fair and prudent to give the seller another chance but not indefinitely so. In this situation the seller hopes that by continuing the buyer has waived or foregone his right to terminate. The buyer may notify the seller of his intention to continue and in so doing seek to reserve his rights, including those of termination. It is certainly unsatisfactory and risky for the seller to carry on spending money with the Sword of Damocles hanging over his head.

5. Liquidated damages

Generally the seller's liability for damages is unlimited and in the ultimate situation a court would fix the amount of damages following presentation of the arguments regarding foreseeability and having seen evidence of real financial damage suffered by the buyer. However, it is open to the parties to fix this sum themselves when they make the contract. This 'liquidated damages' is thus a reasonable pre-estimate of the likely level of damage potentially to be suffered by the buyer in the event of delay. Having agreed the sum and fixed it within the contract the damages are then payable in the event of delay, whether or not the buyer actually suffers any damage, nor does he have to offer any proof of damage being incurred. Thus each party takes a risk. The buyer takes the risk that the amount so fixed would indeed cover his actual loss but gains in return a much more ready means of securing payment for damages. The seller takes the risk that if he is late he will almost certainly have to pay whether or not the buyer is harmed, but in return his liability is limited to the amount predetermined.

Since delay in most cases will cause a buyer to suffer increasing damage as time goes by, liquidated damages clauses generally provide for a certain amount (or percentage of the price of the goods in delay) to be paid per week (or other period) to a maximum period and/or maximum amount.

To be effective liquidated damages clauses must be properly constructed and must satisfy the rule of reasonable pre-estimation. Liquidated damages which are set so high or that cut in so rapidly that their effect is obviously penal rather than compensatory will not be enforceable (at least not by the courts!) nor will penalty clauses which masquerade as liquidated damages.

6. *Force majeure*

If the seller is late he is liable for damages and his contract is open to termination by the buyer. Lateness is not performing the contract by the due date. Thus, one way to avoid these risks is for the due date to be extended. It can be extended by agreement or by some automatic mechanism. If the contract is late the prudent buyer is unlikely to simply agree to an extension as in doing so he waives his rights to damages and to terminate. He may do so in return for some valuable consideration but in the normal course of events there is nothing in it for him to extend. Thus agreement by the buyer should not be seen as having much chance of success if the contract runs into delay. Much better is to have an automatic mechanism. This is the concept of 'Force Majeure' or 'Excusable Delays' clauses, which automatically entitle the seller to more time if delay is caused by events which the parties could not have intended to be within his risk when the contract was made.

This concept indeed is a form of risk sharing. One side or the other will carry the risk of delay caused by particular events. Ostensibly the entire risk lies with the seller. A force majeure clause moves part of the risk to the buyer. Therefore the parties must agree which force majeure events lie with the buyer. There are two approaches. The first is to say that the seller is entitled to more time if delayed by any event beyond his reasonable control. The second is to list the particular events. The advantage of the former to the seller is that it appears wide embracing, the disadvantage is that because it is vague it is inevitably open to dispute which compromises the principle of risk sharing. If a list is given, at least there should be no question as to the application or not of the clause to the particular event. The list typically includes fire, flood, war, riot, insurrection and industrial action (ie inaction!). It should be remembered that the effect of a force majeure clause is usually to allow only more time, not more money. This is legalistically sound, as to allow more money would be inappropriate since many of those risks are insurable in terms of financial consequence and the opportunity of more money would not motivate the seller to avoid these risks or to mitigate their effect in practice.

Two special categories of force majeure are delays caused by suppliers and the customer himself. The seller may well feel that the acts or omissions of suppliers which delay the work are outside his control, but it would be risky to assume that force majeure includes supplier problems unless the clause specifically says so. As far as delays caused by the customer are concerned it is as well not to treat this as force majeure as such. This is because force majeure offers only more time. If the customer is in default he should be obliged to grant the seller more time and more money.

Often it is thought that force majeure clauses should go hand in hand either with 'time is of the essence' contracts or with those that include liquidated damages. While it is true that customers may be more inclined to concede a force majeure clause in either of these situations, and while it is true that these clauses are seen by some as implying greater risk, the key principle is just one of risk. That is, the prudent seller should seek force majeure in all contracts but particularly those where there is a significant risk of delay regardless of the precise language of any of-the-essence, liquidated damages, termination or purchase in default clauses.

7 Delivery incentives

This chapter has so far concentrated on exploring ways of avoiding, or limiting the effect of, the risk of delay, it being taken as read that from the commercial perspective the seller is bound to see a firm contractual commitment to meet a specified time frame as inherently bad news, albeit that consistently delivering on time is very good for customer satisfaction and company reputation. However, every cloud has a silver lining and the requirement to hit a particular deadline can be an opportunity as well as a threat (Figure 6.2).

figure 6.2 Delivery Commitment

Threat	Opportunity
- Termination	- Bonuses
- Damages	- Customer satisfaction
- Reputation	- Reputation

Convincing the customer that meeting urgent delivery requirements implies special measures, greater cost and more management attention can be converted into higher prices or a bonus arrangement of some sort. A bonus might be fixed or variable amounts or percentages of the price which are linked either to hitting an exact deadline or to achieving performance within a specified time frame band.

A delivery incentive scheme can also be combined with the cost incentive scheme described in Chapter 4, as shown in Figure 6.3.

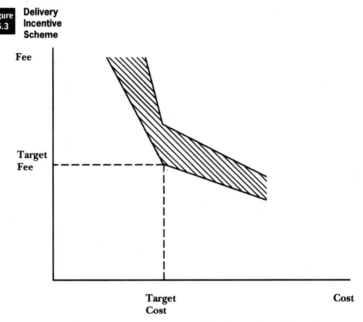

figure 6.3 Delivery Incentive Scheme

Thus in addition to the cost-risk sharing principle the company would be entitled to earn delivery bonuses, perhaps (as in the scheme shown) as a percentage of the cost fee earned. This is very similar to the technical performance bonuses described in Chapter 5 and again allows the company to carry out cost benefit trade-offs between efficiency and time frame of performance.

The Do's and Don'ts of Time Frame Risk

RISK – THE CUSTOMER DELAYS THE WORK.

Do
a) Use the contract to identify all the obligations on the customer.
b) Include a provision to modify the contract in the event of customer default.
c) Specify the periods within which the customer must give relevant approvals.
d) Ensure that any right of the customer to direct or alter the work is provided for in the contract.
e) Promptly report any customer-caused delay to the customer.
f) Pursue claims against the customer if he causes delay.

Don't

a) Accept clauses which absolve the customer from liability for his own acts and omissions.

b) Agree that acts or omissions of the customer are without consequence.

It is important to ensure that the contract specifies clearly all of the obligations of both sides to the bargain. It is easy to fall into the trap of thinking that the contract records a long list of duties on the seller, while the buyer's obligation is limited to paying. Frequently the customer has obligations over and above this; typically these might include the obligation to:

1) Provide materials
2) Provide facilities
3) Provide information and data.

It is essential wherever materials, facilities or data are to be provided by the customer that the contract specifies such things in detail including the date(s) required, the periods over which they are to be provided, their state and location, responsibility for transport or transmission, a general warranty from the customer that the items are fit for purpose, and any financial details including insurance. Patently, any failure in a contractual duty on the part of the customer in complying with these detailed obligations can give a right to the company for an extension in time for contract performance and possibly an increase to the price. This right is best expressed as a definite contract clause as it is generally easier to rely upon an express remedy than an implied one.

Beyond the obligation to provide things, the customer may well be required to do things such as commenting upon or approving/rejecting designs, data, documents, stage completion certificates, plans, specifications, deliveries and invoices. Again, every such obligation must be precisely stated including the time frame within which the obligation must be discharged.

Similarly, if the customer seeks the right to vary the work or otherwise direct the company as to the method of performance, then that right should be stated including any limitations (eg that the customer cannot vary the work so as to cause a reduction in contract value of more than 10 per cent) and the circumstances within which the right can be exercised (eg in the event of ambiguity between different specifications or other documents incorporated in the contract). The consequences of exercising that right must be stated which, surprise surprise, are more money and more time for the company.

As with all claims, the events giving rise to the claim and any resultant claim must be brought promptly to the attention of the customer. Apart from the company's general duty to mitigate the effect of delay, the contract clauses which provide these remedies for the company may place obligations to report such problems and there may be time limitations within which claims may be brought.

Clearly it would be unwise to accept contract clauses which absolve the customer from liability for his own acts or omissions and yet such clauses are used. The justification for this is that the company is on notice that it carries the entire responsibility for and risk in performing the contract. Taken to the extreme this would be absurd. If the customer issues a 'stop work order' (a common provision in US contracts) then the supplier can hardly be expected to complete the work according to the original time frame. On the other hand the company should not be entitled to more money and more time every time the customer 'opens his mouth'. Hence the need for a balanced approach as to the extent the company can claim for more time/money as against the customer being reasonably liable for his acts and omissions.

Notwithstanding any contractual provisions, the company must avoid absolving the customer from liability for his acts and omissions as they arise in the everyday course of dealings between them. For example, the company's project manager, on hearing that the customer is going to be late in discharging one of his obligations, should not say 'Don't worry, we were going to be late anyway'!

RISK – SUPPLIERS DELAY THE WORK.

Do

a) Select suppliers on the basis of proven reliability and performance as well as cost.
b) Give purchasing/subcontract management high visibility and status within the company.
c) Ensure that purchasing/subcontract management are involved in bidding/winning/performing the customer contract.

d) Identify key suppliers at the outset and accord them special attention.

e) Make suppliers aware of the full consequences of lateness.

f) Make suppliers contractually liable for consequential damages.

g) Include supplier default expressly or impliedly in any force majeure clause with the customer.

h) Include the right to terminate for default or cancel for convenience.

Don't

a) Accept limitations of liability from suppliers.

b) Fall for the 'I'm only a poor supplier' routine.

c) Direct suppliers.

Delivery performance by suppliers is a major risk in many projects or other commercial enterprises. Some are suited to Just in Time procurement strategy where the business operation is relatively repetitive and the immediate benefits (low/zero stock, reducing inventory costs in the balance sheet, no storage space required for materials/components) outweigh the obvious risk. Just in Time procurement is usually run hand in hand with partnership sourcing resulting in a small number of (hopefully) reliable suppliers. The risk to the company may be assessed as high impact, low probability and therefore the risk is taken provided effort is devoted to the sound management of the chosen suppliers. In this context management does not mean controlling and directing but liaising, problem solving, mutual quality assurance etc. Whether Just in Time, partnership sourcing or otherwise suppliers are a risk, which demands that the contractual terms and management of suppliers are appropriately addressed. This is examined in Chapter 7.

RISK – THE COMPANY DELAYS THE WORK.

Do

a) Include the right to vary the time for performance.

b) Include force majeure.

c) Involve the customer in the work.

d) Avoid clear commitments to delivery dates.

e) Avoid 'of the essence' commitments.

Don't

a) Give promises that can't be met.
b) Give advance notice of delay.
c) Assume concessions will be granted.
d) Necessarily accept liquidated damages or other 'penalty' clauses.

If the company delays the work it is only for one of two reasons. Either it wants to delay or it cannot help delaying. It might want to delay for a variety of reasons:

1) In order to divert materials, goods or personnel to more urgent or more profitable orders.
2) In order to take advantage of forthcoming falling material prices.
3) In order to absorb personnel coming free from other projects who might otherwise leave.
4) In order to keep the project team together pending receipt of a follow-on contract.
5) In order to release deliveries, sales or profits in line with business requirements.
6) To conceal problems allowing more time for their resolution.

The very best way to have this flexibility without exposing the normal risks consequent upon delay or default is to build into the contract the right to deliver or perform at the company's discretion. This will be totally unacceptable to the customer in many, but not all, cases. It is always worth trying. Its purpose is not necessarily to defeat, such as the Sale of Goods Act implied undertaking to deliver in a reasonable time, it is only to permit the company a sensible degree of flexibility in the many situations where timeliness of performance is not that important.

In the absence of a clause which allows the company to vary the performance then all delay, in the customer's eyes, is down to the company, regardless of it being desire or event that produces the delay. Thus a force majeure clause offers some protection. More pragmatically, or deviously, depending upon point of view, blame may be attributable directly to the customer through his default or indirectly to him by his having given direction to the company or been involved in decision making or otherwise embroiled in events which, it can be said, show the customer approving or concurring with delay, or of condoning failures or omissions of the company.

Of course delay and phrases such as 'of the essence' are only meaningful expressions if the contract specifies dates at or by which performance is to have occurred. If the contract is silent, ambiguous or vague then it is hard for the customer to demonstrate delay. Provided there is no other relevant material, such as a price quotation giving delivery information, which would indicate the intent of the parties, then the customer must rely on the 'reasonable period' of the Sale of Goods Act. If this line is to be followed then care must be taken as, for example, the ambiguity must be clearly ambiguous! A delivery date expressed only as a 'target' may perhaps be ambiguous. The seller might feel that a target is only something at which to aim, there being no great penalty for missing by an inch or a mile. The buyer or a court might think otherwise, that hitting the target is indeed the fundamental purpose and a miss means trouble. Thus a difference of interpretation is not as good as a clear ambiguity, such as the contract referring to different delivery dates for the same thing!

The giving of delivery promises that cannot be met has already been discussed as being sometimes the only way to be considered for a contract. While in the tough commercial world the legitimacy of this can be justified, it must be seen as a measure of last resort as it takes the company into a contract with 100 per cent probability of being late. However, the 'double whammy' with such a contract, or indeed any contract which runs into time difficulties, is the risk of termination for anticipatory breach. Thus care must be taken in providing progress reports and similar material under the contract to customers which forecasts delay. There is a fine balance to be struck between silence, which avoids this risk, and the need to apprise the customer for the purposes of good relationships and to allow the customer the opportunity to mitigate the effect of the delay on himself.

As part of the process of managing delay it is sometimes assumed that customers will agree to concessions or relaxations against the contract requirement on the basis of a preference to have 90 per cent on time rather than 100 per cent six months late. This can be a dangerous assumption unless the contract can be made so as to oblige the customer to approve relaxations. This is an acceptable approach, particularly if the extent of such 'mandatory' relaxations is bounded in some way. Thus the risks consequent upon time delay might be reduced, although there is then the risk that the customer will want some financial consideration for approving the relaxations.

Another question of balance is the desirability or otherwise of contractual 'penalties' such as liquidated damages. If the customer can be 'managed' into accepting delay then it is better not to have liquidated damages in the contract. The presence of such a clause (regardless of its original purpose – penalty or compensation for real anticipated damage) creates a psychological hurdle in persuading the customer to accept late performance. On the other hand, a combination of certainty of lateness and hostile customer can argue for the inclusion of liquidated damages as a means of limiting liability for lateness.

RISK – FORCE MAJEURE DELAYS THE WORK.

Do

a) Ensure that an adequate force majeure clause is included.
b) Ensure that force majeure delays are reported promptly.
c) Ensure that the definition of a force majeure event is understood.

Don't

a) Forget the duty to mitigate.

Whether or not force majeure relief can be implied into the contract, it is always far better to have an express provision which gives the widest possible definition so as to allow the maximum degree of contractual protection. It is important to observe any terms that relate to the availability of that protection, such as a duty to report events within a specified time of their occurrence and to estimate their likely effect. It is also important to ensure that people working on the project understand that this relief is available, that prompt reporting is essential and that the definition of force majeure will be limited in some way so as to exclude many things which might otherwise be thought covered. Force majeure relief does not give 'carte blanche' to sit back while delay mounts. It is a fundamental duty to ensure that steps are taken to eliminate the cause of delay and mitigate its effect.

RISK – THE THREAT OF TERMINATION.

Do
a) Include a period of notice for termination rights.
b) Take all threats seriously.
c) React immediately.
d) Seize the initiative.
e) Take legal advice.
f) Exercise care in all communications.

Don't
a) Assume it's just a bluff.

The first measure of protection against termination is to have the contract require the customer to give notice and permit a period of cure in which the problem can be fixed or proposals made. This should ensure that a termination cannot come completely out of the blue.

However, if the contract is in delay either by due dates for performance having passed or by it being obvious through lack of progress, then unless some relief is available (ie force majeure if the delaying events are covered by such a clause or some act/omission of the customer provided such risk is not within the company's liability), it is the case that the customer is entitled to terminate either by law or under an express contract condition. The risk of termination may be high impact but low probability if the customer's requirement continues to exist and cannot be met more quickly elsewhere. However, that is no reason not to react immediately by getting 'into' the customer to discover his real intentions, his reasons and what might be done to 'buy him off' if he is serious and the threat cannot be nipped in the bud. Indeed, seizing the initiative may be enough in itself to dissuade the customer since immediate, positive pro-active action demonstrates the kind of customer care, the apparent lack of which could possibly be a motivator in the customer having contemplated termination in the first place.

Nevertheless, the threat of termination is most serious and it is prudent to take early legal advice so as to be sure of the formal situation should the customer accept to proceed with such drastic action. Since litigation may ensue it is important to ensure that all communication with the customer, whether oral or written, is handled extremely carefully in case friendly negotiations deteriorate into legal action.

While bluff plays its part in the conduct of commercial negotiations, 'calling the bluff' if termination is threatened can only be considered if there is 110 per cent certainty that it is indeed a bluff. Do not take the risk!

RISK – THE THREAT OF DAMAGES.

Do
a) Treat all potential claims seriously.
b) Consider a counterclaim.
c) Rebut the claim.
d) Limit purchase in default rights.
e) Avoid consequential damages.
f) Create a financial provision.

Don't
a) Agree to liquidated damages payments by deduction.
b) Agree to set-off clauses.
c) Agree to 'discretionary' payments clauses.

If the company is late in performance and cannot pass the responsibility to someone else, then it does face the prospect of a claim for damages from the customer. Thus it should treat all hints of a prospective claim seriously and aim to nip them in the bud. This can be attempted by:

1) Pointing out to the customer that he was wholly or partly to blame (sometimes the thinnest of information can be enough to frighten the customer off).
2) Hinting at the possible consequences eg further delay and disruption as key resources are pulled off the work to assist in defending the claim.
3) Highlighting the possibility of a major counterclaim.

So the objective is to prevent a formal claim being made. Once someone has put a claim on the table it must be assumed that he is serious, believes he can support the claim and intends to see it through. None of these may be true but, on the other hand once a claim is made the claimant is unlikely to simply withdraw it for no other reason than loss of face. If a claim is made then simple rebuttal and the making of a formal counterclaim can be enough to kill the claim off. A tough, firm but well-considered rebuttal may make the customer realise the mountain he must climb in order to succeed and the sheer scale of it, with its implication of bad feelings, diversion of resources to pursue the claim and the cost, may be enough to cause the customer to back off, particularly if it can be made obvious that notwithstanding his degree of resolve, the facts themselves show less than 100 per cent probability of winning. Thus if the rebuttal can draw out facts or opinions not realised by the customer when he formulated his claim, this can be a big disincentive for him to press on.

Similarly, a seriously made, well presented counterclaim may have the same effect. However, whether rebuttal or counterclaim, care must be taken not to reveal all of the company's defences and arguments against the possibility that the customer cannot be dissuaded resulting in the claim possibly becoming a dispute leading to litigation. The company must keep some of its powder dry.

The immediate harm to the company in contract termination may include:

a) Return of monies paid.
b) Write off of costs incurred.
c) Unusable stock.
d) Loss of profits.
e) Loss of overhead recovery.
f) Redundancies.
g) Loss of related business.
h) Loss of confidence and reputation.

This list is bad enough, but after this initial shock wave a second hit may arrive in the form of a damage claim from the customer. As has been seen such a claim can be on the basis of damages flowing directly or consequentially from the company's default. The primary example of the former is any additional cost suffered by the customer in having to purchase elsewhere. Frequently customers will seek to include 'purchase in default' clauses which prima facie are unattractive (to say the least!) but since they only provide a contractual prescription for what the law allows anyway, the introduction of such a clause can be an opportunity to limit purchase in default rights, for example, by specifying a time limit within which the rights must be exercised and by requiring the customer to demonstrate the reasonableness of his actions in purchasing elsewhere and in containing his own costs in pursuit of that end. Since consequential costs such as the customer's own loss of business are only claimable from the company if an express contract condition conveys that liability, or if such loss were reasonably foreseeable by the company, then the company must avoid those clauses and also avoid allowing itself to be put into a position where the customer could argue that his damages were foreseeable by the company. Thus the company should act the 'I'm only a supplier' role and not be too interested in the use to which the customer will put his goods.

Finally, wherever the possibility of a financial settlement arises a provision should be put into the books of account.

When a claim is made the first question in the claimant's mind is how easily he can get the money from the other side. Thus the company should have it in mind when negotiating the contract in the first place to avoid making it possible for the customer to have a simple means to take its money. There are three main clauses to watch out for. Firstly, if the issue is one of liquidated damages, then avoid clauses which allow payment of liquidated damages to the customer to be made automatically following lateness by deduction against outstanding or future invoices. Ideally, the method of settlement should be left to the company, allowing it to choose how and when to pay if the customer were ever in the position of conceding a liquidated damages claim. Secondly, contract clauses which allow the customer to set off one alleged debt against another liability (ie by reducing payment on another contract in the sum of the claim to which it feels entitled) should be avoided. Finally, there is danger in those payments clauses which allow the customer at his discretion to reduce or suspend payments in the event of his not being satisfied with the progress or performance of the contract.

chapter 7

Supplier risk

1 For the want of a nail!

For the want of a nail the battle was lost!

Many projects rely on the performance of a key supplier or suppliers. To rely on somebody else in any endeavour is to take a risk. On the other hand it is said that placing part of the work, and thereby implicitly delegating responsibility for that work, with suppliers is to 'spread the risk around'.

So is risk taken, or spread or both, and if the latter, where then does the balance lie?

If the battle was lost for want of a nail then was it lost because the supplier of nails failed to supply, was late in supplying or supplied on time but his product failed? If the product failed did it fail against its specification, did it fail against the user's reasonable expectation or did it fail because it was subjected to abnormal and unforeseeable stress in its user application? In any event the user or customer said the battle was lost for want of a nail. Did the supplier accept this allegation? Did it go to court? If fault lay with the supplier, how far was he 'liable', as opposed to being merely 'responsible'? Did he just replace the nail, or was he sued for the loss of kingdom and crown? Perhaps it did not matter because everybody was dead anyway or, to drag the analogy back to the real world, perhaps supplier and/or buyer went out of business as a result.

These questions could only be answered by reference to the contract terms (express or implied) between customer and supplier and hence the bearing or sharing of risk as between the two is a proper avenue for exploration in this book.

One approach to examining risk mitigation in the out-sourcing of work would be simply to say that the inverse of every other rule in the book should be applied. This would be quite legitimate but would be a poor substitute for a proper analysis as the perspectives of purchasing as an end customer and of purchasing where the purpose is to 'sell on' or otherwise make use of the purchase in another transaction, can be quite different. As this book generally concentrates on the latter perspective the risk of failure attributable to suppliers in achieving that purpose is worthy of review.

 Suppliers and subcontractors

A convenient, but sometimes misleading distinction, can be drawn between suppliers and subcontractors. The distinction can mislead because having adopted two descriptions there is sometimes an implication that subcontractors are more important than suppliers, which may or may not be so in the particular circumstances.

Before discussing this further let the following definitions be postulated:

Supplier : An out-source which provides standard items at catalogue prices according to standard conditions of contract

Subcontractor : An out-source which provides customised work at negotiated prices according to contract conditions which are negotiated and/or reflective of the end customer's conditions

There are some important points here. Looking at the definition of a supplier there are some variables within the definition. The items might be partly customised, the prices might be negotiated to some extent (eg best customer or volume discounts) and the standard conditions might be the seller's or the buyer's dependent upon a number of things (eg custom and practice, relative bargaining positions). Turning to the definition of subcontractor the degree of customisation, price negotiation or reflection of the end customer's conditions can vary greatly from project to project.

A supplier receives a 'purchase order', a subcontractor receives a 'subcontract'.

Notice also that monetary value is not mentioned at all in the definitions. A purchase order can be of much greater value (eg high quantity of high cost items) than a subcontract (eg providing one small area of specialism) but be less important because the items are readily available elsewhere. Conversely, a small value purchase order for an item on the project critical path can assume much greater importance than a major subcontract, the activities of which have plenty of 'float' in the project plan.

So the different terminology can imply different degrees of importance which is certainly misleading. The crucial point is that out-sources which are key to the success of the project must be singled out and given special treatment.

Out-sourcing benefit v risk

The question must be asked, does the buyer want to take the risk at all? It might be less risky to undertake all the work of the contract in-house. Inevitably much out-sourcing has no practicable alternative. The manufacturer of washing machines is probably not also in the business of producing copper wire, rubber hosing, widgets (the device that causes the machine to fail a day outside its warranty!) or many of the other components which together are built into a complete machine. However, it may be in his interests to fabricate the drum himself. Clearly the cost/benefit (where benefit includes risk sharing) analysis must be done before a decision is made.

In this context the expression 'out-sourcing' is used simply as a term that embraces suppliers and subcontractors. The expression is frequently used to describe the more complex process of acquiring externally a major service which is usually performed by an internal department. For these purposes the more simple usage will suffice although the advice given here, in so far as risk management is concerned, is equally applicable to the complex application. The alternative expressions of 'purchasing' or 'procurement' are avoided as these do not seem to carry the weight of importance that the activity deserves.

In out-sourcing a number of questions of principle are usually considered in determining strategy. Provided it seems like a good idea and the market can probably provide the required quantity, quality and specification, then the three questions are selection method, pricing regime and contract strategy. It is not the task of this book to explore all the aspects of out-sourcing strategy but an outline appraisal of the balance of risk in each of the three points of principle (Figure 7.1) is appropriate. So if the decision path towards out-sourcing is perhaps as shown at Figure 7.2, then the risk appraisal can be seen at Steps 3 and 6 (Figure 7.2).

 **Three Strands of Out-sourcing Strategy**

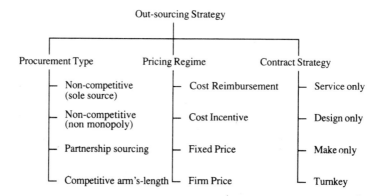

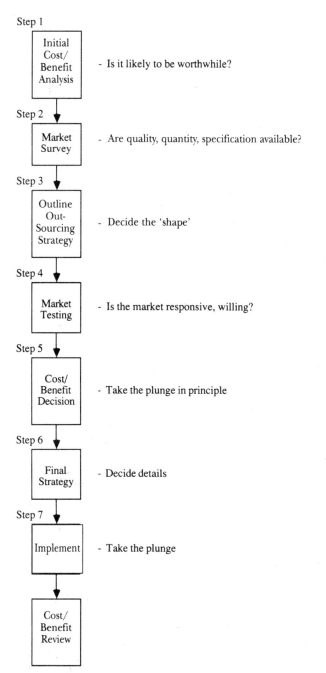

figure 7.2 Deciding to Out-source

Step 1
Initial
Cost/
Benefit
Analysis — - Is it likely to be worthwhile?

Step 2
Market
Survey — - Are quality, quantity, specification available?

Step 3
Outline
Out-
Sourcing
Strategy — - Decide the 'shape'

Step 4
Market
Testing — - Is the market responsive, willing?

Step 5
Cost/
Benefit
Decision — - Take the plunge in principle

Step 6
Final
Strategy — - Decide details

Step 7
Implement — - Take the plunge

Cost/
Benefit
Review

Taking these three principles in turn it is possible to visualise where the balance of advantage lies. In each of Figures 7.3, 7.4 and 7.5 the relationship is shown between buyer control of the supplier and the level of risk which the buyer delegates to the supplier.

figure 7.3 **Procurement Type**

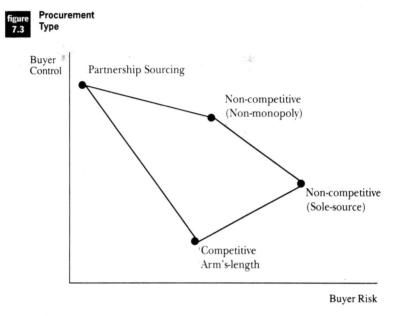

Figure 7.3 illustrates the wisdom of partnership sourcing against competitive arm's-length buying. In partnership sourcing the buyer has greater control through communication, openness and cooperation which are the principles of that philosophy. In competitive arm's-length procurement control is much more limited as the nature of the transaction militates against it. This is particularly so as in the former, companies have a small number of partnership sources where in the latter a large number of suppliers is the norm. In partnership sourcing there is time to talk to and influence the supplier, in competitive arm's-length there is not. However, partnership sourcing does not mean that the buyer has reduced his supplier risk to zero. Apart from the fact that things can and do go wrong no matter the nature of the transaction, partnership sourcing in itself is not a perfect answer. Partnerships in supply, just as in all other partnerships, can suffer from complacency and over familiarity. The aim must to be to ensure that the commercial objectives of the two sides to the bargain are as much in

harmony as possible and partnership sourcing is certainly an improvement over the tough but simple alternative of arm's-length contracting, where the respective objectives can easily come into conflict. Sound partnership sourcing, however, retains a competitive element, either as a 'threat' that the work could go elsewhere when the order is due to be renewed, or by maintaining two or more partnership sources for the same products.

The generally much less desirable alternative to both partnership and arm's-length competitive sourcing is the selection of a non-competitive supplier. The term 'non-competitive' in this sense is used to mean selected without competition rather than un-competitive, as in unattractive on price or other grounds. Non-competitive sourcing is used where there is only a single source of supply, urgency precludes the time taken by competitive selection or where constructing the basis for a competition seems too difficult or impracticable. Whatever the reason the end result for the buyer is the same. Less control and more risk as the supplier, who essentially enjoys a captive customer, is not motivated to heed the wishes of the buyer or to perform in such a way as to minimise risk to the buyer. After all, if things do not work out quite right, the buyer has little alternative but to stick with the supplier until things come good.

This is perhaps too black-and-white a picture. The advantage of a non-competitive supplier is that he may feel much more motivated to provide a long-term commitment to support the buyer's needs and it is in his interest to increase his business with this particular captive buyer which, in the final analysis, is still best achieved by delivering quality product on time at good prices and responding to the buyer's needs.

Nevertheless, before deciding on a procurement strategy it is as well to consider the general shape of the illustration at Figure 7.3 and determine where within that general envelope the optimum strategy lies, taking heed of the particular situation.

Similarly, Figure 7.4 shows that the choice of pricing regime also has no perfect solution. The buyer must make the choice as to which pricing regime best suits the particular circumstances. For clarity the following definitions apply:

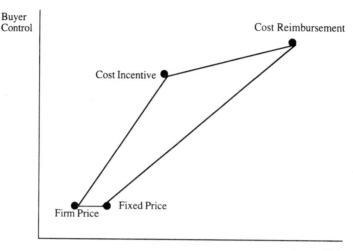

Pricing Regime

Firm Price	: A price which is not variable for any reason (other than change in specification, quantity or time for performance).
Fixed Price	: A price, the final value of which is fixed by reference to some variable parameter such as an inflation index (eg Variation of Price 'VOP' or Contract Price Adjustment 'CPA' arrangement) or a currency exchange rate fluctuation mechanism.
Cost Incentive	: A price based on the supplier's actual costs but with buyer and seller sharing underspends or overspends against a pre-agreed target cost.
Cost Reimbursement	: A price based on the supplier's actual costs plus a pre-determined amount or percentage by way of profit.

A firm price often most suits the buyer as it offers him maximum protection against cost increases, no matter what the cause, whether the cause is simply the effect of inflation or whether the cause is poor estimating by the supplier in the first place. On the other hand, if the work is so incapable of proper estimation, it could be as well for the buyer to swallow the bitter pill of a cost reimbursement arrangement (subject perhaps to a maximum price) with his supplier than to face an endless stream of claims for price increases resulting from inevitable changes in the requirement.

figure 7.5 **Contract Strategy**

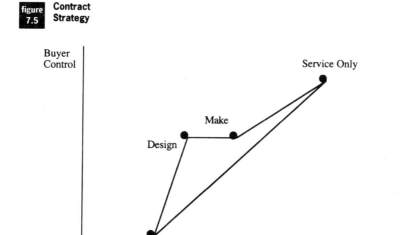

Similarly, with contract strategy the buyer must make his choice as to the degree of control he seeks to exercise over the supplier and the risk he is prepared to take. Figure 7.5 provides in some ways the best example of the principle which is being made here. It may very well be that the buyer considers that, overall, risk to his project is minimised by retaining maximum control of suppliers by purchasing only a service or by letting segments of the work at a time (eg feasibility, project definition, design, make etc). However, in doing so he has in the contractual sense also retained a degree of risk of failure. It is his decision to use or not use the advice of a consultant (acquired under a service order). It is his decision that the design is mature enough to proceed to the 'make or do' phase. The turnkey approach in which the supplier is responsible for everything has the effect, in that contractual sense, of passing risk to the supplier. So in the context of delegating risk to the supplier the choice must be made between maximum control, which equals retaining the contractual risk and minimum control, which equals delegating the risk. On a case by case basis the former may mean the lower overall risk, or it may not.

The same point can be seen in Figures 7.3 and 7.4. In the first of these the buyer's risk (of poor supplier performance) increases more as he moves away from the partnership approach, although it must be said that the distinction is less clear since it all depends on the terms and conditions agreed between the buyer and supplier. The distinction is once again quite clear with regard to the pricing regime. The more the buyer wishes to control the supplier the more he must move towards a cost reimbursement basis which leaves him with both the risk of cost overruns and of the utility of the supplier's output.

Returning to the question 'Does the buyer want to take the risk at all?' Figure 7.6 puts the question into perspective. The advantages of out-sourcing not only provide the opportunity to share or delegate risk, but also there is the chance to gain additional skills and experience in working with outsiders in areas for which the buyer has little knowledge. Additionally, the buyer and supplier in partnership may well be qualified in terms of resources, capacity and skills base to bid for work for which neither by itself would be qualified or otherwise likely to be in a strong position.

On the down-side out-sourcing means working with a supplier who may be geographically remote, who may have different priorities from those of the buyer and who is not susceptible to local management action by the buyer (in the same way that the buyer's internal activities are subject to control) in the event of problems. All of these things do cause the buyer a burden of management of suppliers which can be costly and on any serious scale at all require a dedicated, expert resource. Putting work out can mean providing jobs for suppliers at the expense of the buyer's own personnel. Finally, no matter how good the contract terms, a supplier can suffer a catastrophic failure causing serious problems for the buyer.

So, great thought must be given whenever the company arrives at its 'make/buy' decision to ensure that all the risks, advantages and disadvantages are taken into account.

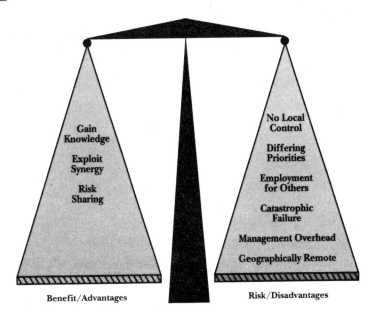

figure 7.6 Out-sourcing Benefit v Risk

Benefit/Advantages

Gain Knowledge

Exploit Synergy

Risk Sharing

Risk/Disadvantages

No Local Control

Differing Priorities

Employment for Others

Catastrophic Failure

Management Overhead

Geographically Remote

4 The do's and don'ts of supplier risk

For the benefit of the English language, in the succeeding paragraphs 'out-sources', whether suppliers or subcontractors, are referred to collectively as suppliers.

In the following it must be said that in most dealings with suppliers it is unlikely to be the case that all of the suggested provisions will be adopted/excluded at the buyer's wish. The recommendations should therefore be seen as a goal to be achieved partially if not in whole. They are not 'all or nothing' recommendations. The degree to which the 'do's' must be achieved depends on the criticality of the items to be supplied. Indeed, suppliers' willingness to accept particular regimes and conditions should be a factor in supplier selection. Also in the real world the respective bargaining positions of the two sides is a factor. Clearly the sole source supplier of a particularly crucial item will be less persuaded to accept some of the recommended clauses than others.

Furthermore, the ownership of risk usually has a price. Hence, to the extent that the recommendations below intend either to transfer risk to the supplier or to emphasise that the risks which are properly his really *do* lie with him, then the issues can enter into the price negotiation. Thus one should always have in mind the cost/benefit trade-off in assessing how far to push some of the points.

RISK – CONSEQUENCES OF SUPPLIER FAILURE.

Do

a) Make the supplier aware in writing pre-contract of the criticality of his work.

b) Reinforce this by putting 'preambles' or 'recitals' in the contract agreement identifying the purpose of the order and the consequences of failure.

c) Remind the supplier in writing from time to time of the importance of his work once the order is under way.

d) Create a relationship with the supplier at senior management level as well as at the buyer/progress chaser level.

e) Include express contract conditions covering the supplier's liability for consequential damages.

Don't

a) Agree to clauses excluding supplier's liability for special or consequential damages.

b) Agree to a financial limit on the supplier's liability under the order.

Compliance with the foregoing should ensure that all consequences flowing from the supplier's failure are foreseeable by him, thus leaving the liability and risk with him. In this context 'failure' means either complete failure (ie the supplier would never perform the work), late performance or partial performance (ie the work is 'completed' but with deficiencies against quality, quantity or specification).

The reason this is important is that normally the supplier is only expected to foresee that his failure would lead to the buyer having to purchase a similar article elsewhere. Thus the liability of the supplier is limited to the extra cost, if any, suffered by the buyer in going elsewhere. The supplier is said to be liable for the immediate financial damage suffered by the buyer flowing directly from the supplier's default. The buyer may, however, suffer additional costs in investigating the availability and effect of alternative articles, he may suffer loss of anticipated profits on the order in hand, he may suffer loss of business as his customers turn elsewhere. These consequential or special damages are not normally recoverable from the supplier unless they were reasonably foreseeable by him and ideally where a contract agreement makes him expressly liable.

RISK – SUPPLIER IS LATE.

Do

a) Specify delivery dates in the order.
b) Emphasise the importance of timely delivery by including 'time is of the essence of the contract' in the order.
c) Require progress reports/forecasts from the supplier.
d) Consider including liquidated damages.
e) Remind the supplier from time to time of the importance of timely delivery.
f) Include a termination for default clause.

Don't

a) Allow submission of progress reports etc to have the effect of gaining acquiescence to late delivery.
b) Allow liquidated damages to eliminate the right to terminate for default.
c) Delay in reserving rights or taking action against the supplier in the event of his lateness.
d) Allow *force majeure* or excusable delays clauses.
e) Be the cause of the supplier's delay.

Supplier lateness is an example of supplier failure which is dealt with above and hence these recommendations take that aspect of failure one step further. The risk that lies here is the consequence to the buyer of the seller being late. Supplier lateness can cause the buyer to suffer financial damage. The decision to be made with regard to including a liquidated damages clause is that, although often used as a quasi-penalty arrangement by buyers, such clauses usually have the effect of limiting the liability of the supplier which transfers part of the risk back to the buyer. On the other hand, once such a clause is agreed, the liquidated damages are actually payable in the event of delay, whether or not the buyer is suffering financial damage. This is unlike a damages at large claim where the damage must be real and provable. Hence the need to decide where the balance of advantage lies – automatic but limited liquidated damages or non-automatic but unlimited damages at large. It is all a question of how much risk to pass to the supplier.

The law allows a buyer to terminate an unfulfilled contract but an express termination for default clause in the order is a better option than to rely upon the general law of contract.

RISK – SUPPLIER'S GOODS ARE 'UNFIT' AFTER DELIVERY.

Do

a) Require conformance to a *performance* specification.
b) Specify the examples of the purposes to which the goods will be put.
c) Include an acceptance clause which delays acceptance until the goods are proven in use.
d) Include an express warranty.
e) Say that the supplier's skill and judgement is being relied upon.
f) Retain payment of part of the price until post-delivery obligations are discharged by the supplier.

Don't

a) Agree to exclusions of implied undertakings such as fitness for purpose.

The purpose here is to tie the supplier into post-delivery obligations that survive for a sensible period (as opposed to a standard or notional period). Failure in these obligations allows the buyer to attack the supplier on a number of grounds ranging from breach of contract (failure to meet the specification), non-performance (goods rejected prior to acceptance), breach of implied conditions or warranties (eg fitness for purpose), express warranty and breach of warranties implied by the supplier's skill and judgement.

By analogy, if a customer buys a central heating system from a professional heating company, he can rely upon the goods being fit for purpose and he can rely upon the advice given by the company.

If he buys all the pieces off-the-shelf from a DIY store he can still expect the goods to be fit for purpose but he has made his own judgement as to their suitability for a particular installation. Thus he transfers some of the risk to himself. In commercial transactions the buyer should avoid holding himself out as an expert in the field of the supplier's products and rely instead on the supplier's skill and judgement.

RISK – THE SUPPLIER GOES OUT OF BUSINESS.

Do

a) A financial health check (eg Dunn and Bradstreet) on the supplier beforehand.
b) Require (if appropriate) a parent company guarantee underwriting the supplier's obligations to perform the contract and underwriting the financial liabilities arising thereunder.
c) Require a bond or guarantee from a bank or other third party covering the financial liabilities of the supplier.
d) Include a clause to vest ownership of parts and materials in the buyer as they are allocated to the contract.
e) Include a right of termination exercisable in the event of actual or prospective insolvency, winding-up or bankruptcy.
f) If appropriate, require the supplier to enter into an ESCROW agreement whereby details of his designs are held confidentially by a third party and made available to the buyer in the event that the supplier is unable to complete the order or to provide product support in the future.

Don't

a) Be persuaded by a financially insubstantial or shaky supplier that everything 'will be all right on the night'.

The risk of a key supplier going out of business is a real one. It does happen and the consequences can be dire. These recommendations do provide the best protection as regards dealing with the chosen supplier if he should be so unfortunate as to get into financial difficulties.

RISK – YOU DON'T KNOW WHAT THE SUPPLIER IS DOING.

Do

a) Require the supplier to provide plans, reports and appropriate documentation and data to provide reasonable visibility of progress.
b) Hold progress review meetings.
c) Use Quality Assurance surveillance to check on progress.
d) Employ an expert in the field of the supplier's work to monitor and advise on progress.
e) Include a 'no waiver' clause.

Don't

a) Allow that receipt, approval or acceptance of any document abrogates the liability of the supplier to fully perform the contract.
b) Allow that progress meetings or the minutes thereof have the effect of altering or varying the order or of condoning non-compliancies or lateness by the supplier.

The essence of this is that it is necessary to provide for visibility and monitoring of progress without that process in itself causing the buyer to accept responsibility for the acts or omissions of the supplier.

Other than in special circumstances the buyer should seek only to monitor the supplier's activities, not to control or authorise them. To exercise control or to prevent progress until the buyer has authorised particular activities is to transfer risk in the performance of the order back from the supplier to the buyer.

RISK – THE SUPPLIER FAILS TO ACCORD THE ORDER ANY PRIORITY.

Do

a) Motivate the supplier by paying on completion only or, if interim payments are to be made, by allowing that his cash flow can be improved by adherence to a sound milestone payment scheme.
b) Motivate the supplier with expectations of future business, customer awareness of his success etc.

c) Ensure the senior management interface between buyer and supplier is exercised to retain the supplier's attention.

d) Involve the supplier in planning and progress of the activity into which his products merge.

e) Remind the supplier of the contractual and legal remedies available in the event of his default and, as appropriate, invoke those remedies.

Don't

a) Delay in taking steps to encourage a slow supplier to perform.

This risk goes to the heart of the 'out-sourcing' dilemma (see Figure 7.6). Inevitably, the supplier will have a different set of business priorities as compared with the buyer. What is high priority to the buyer may be low priority to the supplier. Even if the priorities are right but the supplier runs into problems it is difficult for the buyer to exercise any local management that will resolve the situation. Certainly, the threat or act of suspending payments if they are of significant magnitude is guaranteed to grab the attention of the supplier at a senior level.

RISK – THE SUPPLIER 'SPILLS THE BEANS'.

Do

a) Include a clause preventing the supplier from making publicity announcements about the order without the buyer's prior written permission.

b) Include a confidentiality clause requiring the supplier to keep confidential the existence of the contract, commercial information (eg prices) associated therewith and all documents and data provided to the supplier for the purposes of the order.

Don't

a) Treat the supplier's information with any less respect than that with which he is expected to treat yours.

Commercial contracts are private matters and should be kept as such. All companies like to make publicity mileage out of securing or delivering a major order. However, the buyer may not want his own thunder stolen by a premature announcement by a supplier. More fundamentally sources of supply may be a valuable commercial secret, special arrangements between buyer and particular suppliers may be a key part of a business, commercial, marketing or bidding strategy. In any of these events there could well be a serious risk to the fortunes of the buyer if such matters are inappropriately revealed. Some trading arrangements which touch upon anti-competitive practice are required by statute to be made public, but such statutory obligations are quite different from the supplier not having a free hand to expose details of arrangements with the buyer.

Documents or data provided to the supplier by the buyer may be proprietary to the buyer or to a third party and should not be used by the supplier for any purpose other than the particular order. To permit otherwise is to risk damage to other interests of the buyer or to expose the buyer to the risk of third party action.

For these reasons it is important that a veil of commercial secrecy is drawn around the transaction.

RISK – THE SUPPLIER DAMAGES YOUR PROPERTY.

Do
a) Include a clause making the supplier liable for physical loss or damage to your property which he causes.
b) Require the supplier to carry adequate insurance cover.

Don't
a) Be talked into carrying the risk because 'your own insurance must cover it'.

While the buyer's own insurance may well cover loss or damage occasioned, for example, by supplier's personnel at the buyer's premises, that should be no reason to excuse him from a contractual liability. If he is not liable, he is less motivated to ensure that his people take due care.

RISK – SUPPLIER PUTS THE WORK ELSEWHERE.

Do
a) Include a 'no assignment' clause.
b) Reserve the right to approve his suppliers.

c) Reserve the right to visit or inspect his suppliers.

d) Require the supplier to 'flow down' (ie include in his purchase orders), those terms and conditions which protect your interests.

Don't

a) Take any liability with regard to the selection or performance of his suppliers.

All the do's and don'ts in this chapter seem perhaps to be mutually exclusive. On reading them it can well seem that if the supplier can be persuaded to accept all the do's (where they relate to the inclusion of contract conditions as opposed to examples of good risk management technique), then it seems most unlikely that he would also accept the don'ts (to the extent that they are contract clauses to avoid, which, if included, would balance the do's clauses, mitigate the supplier's risk and transfer risk back to the buyer). But if generally it seems unlikely that the buyer will accept both do's and don'ts then under this heading it must seem impossible. The supplier would argue that if he is to allow buyer involvement in selection and inspection of his own suppliers, then such interference in the conduct of his business and in the performance of his contract has a price. The price is either a real price (ie he has to charge more for the risk of the buyer being capricious, over-fastidious or tardy in the exercise of such rights), or a contractual price whereby the buyer accepts some, if not all, responsibility for the effect of exercising such rights.

The risk burden v price benefit is discussed earlier in this chapter, but the linkage between involvement and responsibility does not have to be absolute. The buyer must argue that leaving the entire risk in the performance of the order with the supplier is not the same as establishing that all appropriate risk reduction and risk management practices are in place. It is little comfort to the King to know that he can sue the supplier of horseshoes once the battle is lost. Much better for the King (or one of his serfs, the latter-day term for purchasing manager) to have reserved and exercised the right to approve and inspect the horseshoe maker's nail supplier in the first place.

This is not to say that the buyer undertaking these activities should supplant a proper strict duty on the supplier to carefully select and inspect his own suppliers – quite the contrary. The purpose of the buyer taking any interest is to avoid a possible conflict of interests (which equals risk to the buyer). The supplier's main concern may be quick delivery and low cost. The buyer may be more concerned about quality in the general sense of 'goodness', durability and reliability. This raises questions of specification but, in addition to properly specifying the requirement (particularly in performance terms), it can do the buyer no harm to ensure that the order is executed professionally by doing more than implicitly threatening legal action against the supplier if it all goes wrong. Of course such principles apply just as much to the buyer's surveillance of the supplier's intramural activity, but it remains the case that the supplier's suppliers are potentially a weak link in the chain, a risk which the buyer should seek to mitigate.

RISK – THE SUPPLIER 'CAUSES' BREACH OF THE CONTRACT.

Do
a) Include all the 'mandatory flow down' conditions.
b) Negotiate with suppliers pre-contract.
c) Include all other 'protective' conditions.

Don't
a) Forget to secure adequate intellectual property rights (IPR).

It is important to understand the role of suppliers as regards the contract with the customer. Purchase orders with suppliers are not incidental to the contract, they are at the very heart of it. For this reason, as has already been said, suppliers must be made aware in a way that has as much contractual effect as possible on their contribution to the whole. But the supplier cannot know what he does not know. Where the customer requires certain conditions to be included in subcontracts so as to protect his position or so as to acquire certain rights (eg to inspect supplier premises), then it is important to solicit the supplier's agreement to this. Failure to secure that agreement would leave the company in breach of contract with his customer, a situation always to be avoided! This illustrates the benefit of negotiating with potential suppliers prior to contract signature with the customer. Not only does this help to ensure that suppliers will line up with the customer's requirements but, if major difficulties emerge as part of that process, it allows the company at least the opportunity to follow a different line in negotiations with the customer.

To be on the safe side it is as well to 'flow down' all the conditions from the contract with the customer, albeit that all such conditions to be included in subcontracts should where appropriate be 'toughened up'. There is nothing quite as good as having suppliers on a 'shorter rope' than the customer has with the company.

The most significant example of a risk caused by failure to secure the right terms with suppliers is in the area of IPR. Any contract which involves the use of supplier IPR necessarily demands that the company secures rights which as a minimum are adequate to permit performance of the contract. These may range from the simple ability to copy and use supplier software through to the right to sub-licence or assign licences in the supplier's designs or patents to the customer.

Thus, in the context of this risk, if the company fails to secure all the right terms with suppliers, the company may be in breach of the contract in respect of supplier work for which the supplier is not himself in breach of the subcontract.

To put it in a nutshell, the company must take care to secure from the supplier everything necessary to permit compliance with the contract and at the same time to hold the supplier liable for any consequences arising from both breach of the subcontract and, if applicable, consequent breach of the contract.

RISK – THE SUPPLIER'S GOODS ARE NO LONGER WANTED.

Do

a) Include a cancellation for convenience clause.

Don't

a) Agree to pay anticipated profits or compensation for unrecovered overheads.

This is a simple but important risk. In every project there is the chance that the company may want to disengage itself from a particular supplier because, even if the supplier is performing, the goods may have been removed from the customer's requirement or a source of better/cheaper alternative goods may have been discovered elsewhere. In such situations the company must not find itself hide-bound to remain in contract with a supplier for goods which have become unwanted, unattractive or economically undesirable. It is far better to have a cancellation for convenience clause which not only allows the right to cancel but prescribes the financial settlement to be reached between the parties. This is better for the company than having to negotiate the cancellation of the subcontract, with the supplier having the whip hand. Also, the right to cancel for convenience with prescriptive treatment of the settlement does not preclude, for example, the company renegotiating the price (downwards) with the existing supplier under the list of cancellation. The disincentive to exercise a right to cancel which the supplier may seek is an entitlement to payment of anticipated profits and other compensation. This provision should be avoided as, not only are anticipated profits difficult to establish (eg perhaps the supplier was actually expecting to make a loss but would not say so, of course), but the disincentive could be so great as to make the cancellation right worthless.

Other risks

In addition to the foregoing the supplier may be the root cause of actions against the company by third parties who may claim infringement of IPR or damage due to defective products. Both of these will be covered in Chapter 8.

Post-delivery risk

Is there life after delivery?

The seller wants to deliver, take the money and run. The buyer wants the goods, doesn't want to pay and hopes to have a stranglehold on the seller forever! Somewhere between these two extremes there is a reasonable position regarding post-delivery obligations. In a clinical sense both sides should be seeking certainty as to the point at which the contract has been wholly performed in return for which the full contract price is payable. There may well be residual obligations on the seller after this point in terms of supporting the delivered products, but the real risk lies in the question as to whether all liability in the material work has or has not passed to the buyer.

Key contractual milestones

There are several important points to consider:

Inspection : The opportunity for the buyer to verify that goods offered in the performance of the contract comply with the requirements of the contract.

Delivery : The point at which the contract is performed (regardless of the passage of property and risk), whether by physical movement of goods or by paperwork transaction.

Passing of Property :   The transfer of legal title in the goods from seller to buyer.

Passing of Risk   :   The transfer of liability from seller to buyer for loss or damage to the goods.

Rejection   :   The right of the buyer to reject goods which do not comply with the requirements of the contract.

Acceptance   :   The point at which the buyer concurs that the contract has been performed, forever extinguishing his right to reject.

Warranty   :   A period after delivery during which the seller has express or implied liability to the buyer for defects in the goods.

Payment   :   Settlement of the contract by the buyer in return for the contract having been performed.

Not surprisingly, buyer and seller have exactly opposing views in each of these principles (Figures 8.1 and 8.2).

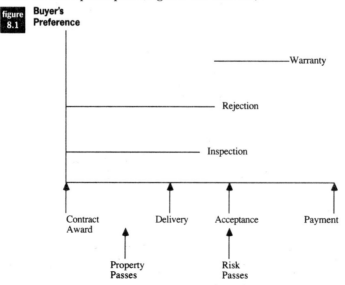

figure 8.1 Buyer's Preference

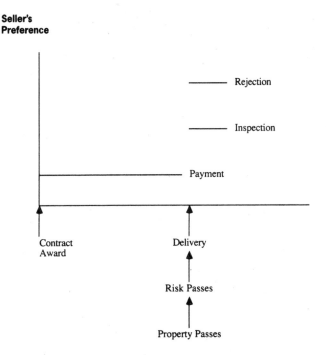

figure 8.2 Seller's Preference

Rejection

Inspection

Payment

Contract Award

Delivery

Risk Passes

Property Passes

So the buyer likes the ability to inspect the work throughout the period of the contract exposing a risk of rejection even before the seller has offered performance. He wants early title to parts, materials and finished goods and wants to pay way after delivery, having delayed acceptance and adoption of loss/damage risk as long as possible. The seller on the other hand sees performing the contract as his private business until he offers performance, where transfer of property and risk should transfer simultaneously with acceptance immediately thereafter (if not concurrently with) and having enjoyed payment over the life of the contract achieving 100 per cent of the price on or before delivery.

These things must all be worked out in the detail of the contract negotiation. The inter-linking of delivery, property and risk are all dealt with in the choice of arrangements set out in 'Incoterms' which are particularly useful for export contracts. Probably the most important event from the seller's perspective is achieving contractual acceptance. This is because, if goods are legitimately rejected then, unless compliant goods can be offered within the period allowed, the seller is in fundamental breach and risks the contract being terminated for default. Once acceptance has occurred then the right to reject has disappeared, the risk of termination has evaporated and the buyer can only pursue the seller under express or implied warranties if there are any problems with the goods.

Thus the definition, scope and timing of acceptance is something upon which to focus much attention in contract negotiation and in execution of the contract. Getting the customer to 'accept' things is good commercial risk management, such as the classic separation of 'design' and 'make' whereby if the customer accepts the design prior to the make/build/implement stage, he will have much greater difficulty in seeking redress from the supplier at the later stage if there are problems associated with the design.

 Residual obligations and risks

Depending on the construction of the agreed contract, primary post-delivery risks may therefore include (if reference is made to Figure 8.1):

1) Rejection of the goods.
2) Goods lost or damaged.
3) Deficiencies discovered under warranty.
4) Payment not made.

These are dealt with later on in this chapter and the risks of non-payment are also examined in Chapter 4. However, the question remains as to what other risks remain with the seller even once the primary risks identified above have been eliminated. Such residual obligations typically cover:

1) Supply of additional goods under contract options.
2) Delivery of technical data and licences for the use thereof.
3) Settlement of outstanding purchase orders, subcontracts, rental agreements, lease agreements etc.
4) Disposal of residual material within the terms of the contract.
5) Resolution of outstanding claims and disputes.
6) Disposal of customer owned property made available for the purposes of the contract.

7) Cancellation/closure of outstanding bonds, guarantees, credit facilities.

8) Termination of teaming, collaboration, consortium agreements.

9) Final negotiation and conclusion of any special pricing arrangements (eg cost risk sharing schemes, VOP adjustments).

10) Establishment of contractual, management and procedural arrangements to provide support services and maintenance of technical skills and data.

11) Application for patents and other forms of intellectual property protection in respect of the work of the contract.

Secondary duties such as these, which do not go to the heart of the contract but nevertheless form part of the entire set of contract obligations, are very important. Whether they relate to obligations owed directly to the customer or to other parties they can be easy to overlook. The arrival of a letter from the customer two years after the contract is finished, legitimately exercising a contract option for more goods which the company had entirely forgotten about, can be an alarming experience. This is particularly so if the goods are no longer in production or no longer capable of economic production. Similarly, a late but proper invoice from a supplier which arrives after the books have been closed on the contract and the profit released to the Profit and Loss Account can be disappointing and certainly risky for the project or contract manager, who must explain this to the finance director!

Just as it is important to plan the start up and execution of a contract, so it is important to plan the closure of the contract. Good administrative procedures should ensure that these residual obligations are not forgotten and positive action should be taken to discharge or eliminate them. For example, the contract option which survives completion of the main work should be examined for viability and if there is a risk that the option could not be performed at all, or not at a profit, then early action should be taken to persuade the customer to agree that the option right is deleted or perhaps to reduce the length of the period during which the option can be exercised.

In business as in life there are more people who are good at starting things than there are people who are good at finishing things. This is a characteristic which is also true of companies. Therefore great attention must be paid to ensuring that residual obligations are effectively dealt with one way or another.

4 Pricing

When a price is formulated for a potential contract usually only two things are considered. Will this price win the contract? Will this price cover the cost, leaving something for profit? The 'top down' examination of price in terms of perceived competitiveness against the opposition needs to converge against the 'bottom up' approach to estimating cost, together with the business expectation as to the level of profit. However, part of the process of pricing must look at what allowances should ideally be made for risk (see also Chapter 3) being both technical and commercial in character. As with all risks the key questions are impact and probability. The probability axis includes a time dimension in terms of the period for which the company is exposed to the risk. Thus risk allowances should include consideration of the timing of acceptance, the period of rejection, the start and length of warranty. In addition to considering the timing, scope and scale of the primary post-delivery risks are important. So, too, is the taking into account the scope, scale and risk dimensions of the residual obligations.

5. Account management

Every risk is an opportunity. The primary and residual risks that lie at the tail end of the contract are very real and need to be carefully managed. Eliminating the risks, for example, of late delivery and deficient goods means not only a greater chance of completing the contract at the anticipated level of profit but it also means a satisfied customer. Needless to say, satisfied customers are more likely to come back for more and the company's reputation will have grown in the market place. Thus the contract should not only be seen as the mountain of obligations and risks but as the opportunity to make profit and secure further orders. This much is a blinding glimpse of the obvious but many companies fail to take the opportunity at the start of the contract, or even beforehand, to work out how the particular contract can be used to generate more business. A 'product plan' may look at the technical evolution of a product, how and when it will come to the market, the investment needed, the likely customer base, target selling prices and margins, the volume, time frame and phasing of orders and particular major potential orders may feature as key milestones, but this is inevitably a little bit too general. What is needed is a specific plan for the exploitation of the particular contract which looks at the tactics and timing of introducing to the customer ideas for improvements, enhancements, upgrades, maintenance and other support services. Indeed these opportunities may grow out of problems and risks encountered during the contract, or anticipated to emerge post-delivery. The problem at the end of the contract of holding open an option for the customer to purchase more goods which at that time (unlike at the time of the contract, some years earlier perhaps) are expected to be uneconomic of further production, can be turned into the opportunity to have the customer consider newer, better products as an alternative – subject of course to some renegotiation of the prices!

6. The do's and don'ts of post-delivery risk

RISK – THE GOODS ARE NOT ACCEPTED.

Do
a) Ensure the contract has an acceptance clause.
b) Ensure acceptance occurs on
   i) A specific event
or ii) The elapse of a stated period of time from delivery.
c) Seek acceptance in stages.
d) Ensure that events are clearly documented to evidence acceptance.

Don't
a) Agree to acceptance occurring when
   i) The customer says so
or ii) The goods are taken into use
or iii) The elapse of a 'reasonable' period.
b) Agree to 'delayed' acceptance.
c) Agree to acceptance being linked to payment.

In all contracts it is as well to have an express clause on acceptance. It is such an important milestone that the contract must make it absolutely clear when, where and how acceptance occurs. The best approach is to hang acceptance on to a key event or series of events which are objective and susceptible to clear yes/no, pass/fail criteria. For example, a contract for a complex system could specify a set of 'acceptance tests', the successful completion of which conveys contractual acceptance. The tests may be testing a representative sample of the features demanded in the technical, performance or other specifications which establish the basic requirements of the contract or they may test every feature.

Testing is expensive and in some situations 100 per cent testing is not feasible. Hence once again the principle of risk sharing applies. In the situation just described the customer takes the risk that in accepting the work of the contract in the absence of 100 per cent testing some shortfalls against the contract may exist which are not detected at the acceptance testing stage. Once the work has been accepted his bargaining power and remedies against the seller are much weaker. However, for taking that risk he will have had the benefit of a lower price and perhaps quicker completion and hence the bargain is balanced.

If acceptance testing or something similar is not appropriate the best approach to acceptance is for it to be conveyed at the end of a stated period of time from physical delivery. This simple approach is objective and the length of the period can be negotiated on a case by case basis. A balance will always be struck between the two extremes where the seller would want acceptance to occur concomitantly with delivery, while the buyer would want to suspend acceptance for several years!

Returning to a point touched upon in Chapters 5 and 6, there is the concept of partial performance. If the contract is so constructed to allow for this then it is important that acceptance is conveyed in stages. Thus it is important to spell out in the contract the acceptance arrangements for every item of the contract or every stage of the work. From the seller's perspective the lightest burden of acceptance is clearly preferable and he should look for the simplest approach, certainly as far as an opening position is concerned. For example, he might suggest that acceptance occurs on delivery provided he has submitted a certificate of conformity with the goods.

To back up an objective approach to acceptance it is crucial that the events upon which acceptance depends are thoroughly documented, so as to prevent disputes as to whether acceptance has or has not occurred.

The goal of objectivity is completely frustrated if acceptance is effectively left to the customer's discretion. And yet this is the effect of clauses which say 'the seller shall complete the work in accordance with the contract specifications and to the satisfaction of the buyer'.

Acceptance should be capable of determination without any element of judgement on the part of the buyer or anybody else. Nor should a special piece of paper be needed, such as an 'acceptance certificate' from the buyer. If an acceptance certificate is required to complete, confirm or formalise acceptance then the implication is that the certificate is an essential component of the process or act of acceptance, without which acceptance cannot have occurred. Hence the buyer is hardly going to be motivated to issue a certificate since it is in his interests to delay acceptance for as long as possible.

The uncertainty of the customer 'saying so', is matched by the uncertainty of clauses which provide for acceptance when the goods are taken into use or the elapse of a 'reasonable' period from delivery. Although in the former case, if it is certain that the goods will go into use very quickly (probably so), then it would be beneficial and safe for the seller to agree to acceptance on that basis. In any other circumstance the uncertainty represents a risk. Similarly, references to a reasonable period are inherently risky and only guarantee disputes between the two sides regarding what may be considered a reasonable period in the prevailing circumstances.

The customer's wish to delay acceptance can sometimes be manifested as a clear policy as opposed to a natural instinct. He may specify that acceptance can only take place following extensive use of the goods so that their true utility or performance can be assessed. Clearly this would represent a much greater risk to the seller and one which should be avoided if at all possible.

Finally, it is preferable to avoid the contract linking acceptance to payment. If the arrangements for acceptance are well-defined, resistant to dispute and the criteria represent no major hurdle, then such a linkage is perfectly fine. However, if the burden is onerous it is better that clearing the hurdle does not have the additional complication of cash flow issues surrounding it. However, at the fundamental level if acceptance is not attained due to some deficiency on the part of the seller then the contract has not been performed and the buyer can hardly be expected to pay, although the question of the actual remedies (termination, damages) must depend on the circumstances and the terms of the contract.

RISK – THE GOODS ARE REJECTED.

Do
a) Avoid the contract giving rights of rejection.
b) Link rejection with acceptance.
c) Limit the period within which a rejection can be made.
d) Provide a right of appeal against rejection.
e) Require notice of rejection to be in writing.
f) Seek a right to compensation for invalid rejections.
g) Make sure that property and risk in rejected goods is specified.
h) Prescribe responsibility for returning/redelivering rejected goods.

Don't
a) Forget to lodge appeals.
b) Fail to challenge rejections and interrogate the rejection closely.

In the seller's ideal world the buyer is obliged to accept the work and has no opportunity to reject, thus the correct if somewhat fanciful suggestion that the buyer should have no right of rejection. Assuming therefore that rejection rights must apply the question is how to limit this risk. The concepts of acceptance and rejection go hand in hand and the contract should reinforce the general principle that acceptance extinguishes any right of rejection. Any period within which rejection is allowed should be stated, limited and triggered by some event such as physical delivery. If rejections are allowed, then sensibly there should be a right of appeal as, presumably, if the seller was confident that he delivered conforming goods, there must be some chance that the buyer's purported rejection is invalid. Incidentally, it should be stated that the right of rejection relates only to a belief that the goods genuinely do not conform to the requirements of the contract. There should be no ability to reject the goods on some general grounds of dissatisfaction. A rejection is potentially a very serious situation for the seller and good practice and protocol demand that it is notified formally and in writing within the period allowed.

The consequences of rejection can range from termination of the contract to delay in payment and the additional cost of investigating the rejection. It is therefore reasonable that if rejections are found invalid the buyer should be required to compensate the seller for the effect of these consequences, some of which will have occurred by the time the invalidity is established.

Whether a rejection is ultimately shown to be valid or not, there is a danger that the goods are in a contractual limbo in terms of where lies property and risk and so it is important to make provision for this so that, amongst other things, one side has the loss/damage risk insured. As a corollary the contract should also nominate the party which is to have responsibility for moving rejected goods around.

Sometimes rejection clauses specify a time frame within which appeals have to be lodged. The seller should ensure that he has in place the procedures to trigger the lodging of an appeal very swiftly after receiving notice of a rejection with which he disagrees. It is no good for rejected items to be returned by the customer and left lying in Goods Inwards for several months before anybody notices! Procedures should also exist for handling rejected goods so they do not accidentally (or deliberately!) become re-mixed with other 'good' goods.

RISK – PROPERTY DOES NOT PASS.

Do
a) Ensure the contract has a clause on passage of property.
b) Retain property until the last possible minute.

Don't
a) Agree to 'vesting' clauses.

The key question in the passage of property is the point or time at which it is conveyed and where the balance of advantage lies. On the one hand retaining property in the goods until payment has been made in full (so called Romalpa clauses) gives the company security in so far as, if payment is not made, it still owns the goods and thus its remedy for non-payment would include recovery of the goods for sale elsewhere. On the other hand if the goods are consumable, are inaccessible or likely to have deteriorated since delivery, such a remedy is not that helpful and if property has passed to the customer then a clearer case exists for legal action in respect of payment of the contract price. So the choice inevitably depends on the nature of the goods and the characteristics of the customer.

Part of this equation is the degree to which it is reasonable for property to pass to the customer prior to delivery under so-called 'vesting' arrangements. These are usually sought by the customer in return for granting the facility for advance or interim payments. There is sense in the argument that his security for advancing monies is property in the goods or material parts thereof as they are purchased or allocated to the contract. However, it can be argued that if he has already enjoyed the advantage of a lower price in return for promising advance payments, why should he have the additional benefit of early passage of property in such goods or materials. Setting aside the principle there are two main difficulties with vesting clauses. Firstly, there is the problem of identifying materials or goods in respect of which passage has passed to the customer. This is because of the limitations of accounting systems to provide this sort of facility, complicated by the fact that the company may purchase the same items for many contracts and may have several contracts with many different customers, all of which include vesting clauses. Perhaps the best advice is that if a vesting clause has to be accepted then it should be ensured that it does not allow the customer any rights to verify compliance! The second concern is that care should be taken to ensure that property only passes if advance payments are actually made rather than just promised.

RISK – THE GOODS ARE LOST OR DAMAGED IN TRANSIT.

Do
a) Ensure the contract has a clause on passage of risk.
b) Seek the earliest possible transfer of risk.
c) Arrange appropriate insurance.

Don't
a) Carry risk in the acts or omissions of the customer.

In this context risk simply means the risk of loss or damage to the goods somewhere between acquisition of the component parts and materials by the seller through to the point of physical delivery to or acceptance by the buyer. Each party normally wants the risk to be carried by the other side and so, when the point has been negotiated, the key issue is to ensure that insurance cover is arranged for the period and scope of the risk and that any other arrangements to safeguard the physical security of the material are in place. Although insurance policies may cover the risk of loss or damage caused other than by the seller's own acts or omissions, it is always prudent to have the contract state that the acts or omissions of the buyer are within his own responsibility and liability.

RISK – THE GOODS FAIL AFTER DELIVERY/ACCEPTANCE.

Do
a) Avoid any post-delivery liability.
b) Exclude the provisions of the Sale of Goods Act.
c) Limit the extent and scope of express warranties.

Don't
a) Assume customer dissatisfaction equates to a contractual liability.
b) Agree to warranty bonds or retentions.

The primary objective is to avoid any liability once the contract is complete. Contract completion can mean many different things, but here it is used to convey the idea that performance of the contract has been achieved in so far as delivery is complete and acceptance has been attained. Whilst residual obligations may remain, the primary objective has been secured. Setting aside any residual obligations (eg to maintain the manufacturing drawings) the question is what liabilities arise regarding the delivered goods? If the customer can be persuaded by a lower price or other valuable consideration to accept all the risk once the contract is complete, so much the better. To avoid any risk the contract must achieve three things. Firstly, a clear and comprehensive statement on acceptance. Secondly, an express exclusion of implied warranties and undertakings, including those evoked under the auspices of the Sale of Goods Act. Finally, there must be no express warranty of any sort.

Exclusions of liability must be carefully worded (see Chapter 1) but failure to expressly exclude the SOGA implied undertakings as to satisfactory quality and fitness for purpose mean they do apply unless convincing argument (such as the customer having specified in detail his requirement and how the seller should achieve it), can be mounted to the contrary. These undertakings are ill-defined in scope and time frame and, if only for the sake of certainty, are best excluded in favour of an express warranty if the customer is not willing to carry all the post-delivery risk himself.

The aim of anyone on the seller's side who is responsible for drafting a warranty clause is to so restrict its scope and application as to render it virtually harmless and thus of no risk to the seller. The warranty period and the event (preferably physical delivery or contractual delivery if earlier (eg ex-works) and not acceptance, that starts the warranty clock ticking should be stated and the clause should list all the exclusions, of which the following are possible examples:

1) Goods not covered by the warranty.
2) Goods for which no warranty claim is received within the warranty period.
3) Goods not returned within the warranty period.
4) Goods exhibiting defects other than those which are a demonstrable failure against the contract specification.
5) Goods where the alleged defect is not reproducible by the seller.
6) Goods exhibiting defects likely to be attributable to
   i) Wear and tear
   ii) Improper use, maintenance or storage
   iii) Defective components.

The warranty should also be clear as to whether design and manufacture are both covered. A warranty on manufacturing workmanship and materials means that one product exhibiting such a defect would be covered by the warranty, but a warranty covering the design may require the seller to remedy a defect in an entire consignment even though only one unit may exhibit the defect. Thus the difference between a manufacturing warranty and a warranty covering design as well is the scope and the scale of the risk. If the seller is to be liable under warranty then he must seek to have the choice of remedy within his control. The option to repair or replace or refund money should be his.

Thus it can be seen that a warranty as drafted by the seller, if given a free hand, will produce something of no practical worth to the buyer! It is all part of the game of moving risk around.

Needless to say, therefore, the prudent seller will carefully scrutinise all warranty claims and never assume that it (the product) must be wrong just because the customer says it's wrong. The wary customer will have his own views on warranty obligations and one way for him to impose his view is to demand a warranty retention or bond. The warranty retention means that some part of the contract price will not be paid until the customer is satisfied that all post-delivery problems have been satisfactorily ironed out. The warranty bond allows the buyer to call upon a third party to impart money in his direction if the seller fails to discharge warranty liabilities, notwithstanding that the contract price may have been paid in full.

RISK – TECHNICAL DATA MUST BE HANDED OVER.

Do
a) Avoid any clause granting rights in intellectual property.
b) If unavoidable, deal with the issue with an eye to the future.
c) Grant rights only in deliverable data.
d) Limit the amount of deliverable data.
e) Grant rights only in that work required under the contract.
f) Grant rights in principle only, leaving terms to be negotiated later.
g) Grant rights in the following order
   i) use
   ii) use and copy
   iii) use, copy and modify.
h) Limit rights to the customer only.
i) Include express provisions regarding confidentiality.

Don't
a) Fall for the trap that because the customer has paid he must own all the IPR.
b) Forget to maximise IPR protection by patents etc.

Intellectual Property Rights (IPR) is the greatest asset the company has. The company's unique ideas, skills and reputation are what gives it its products, profits, position in the market place and its competitive advantage. More so than any other asset, it should be jealously guarded. Tangible assets such as plant and machinery which are stolen, damaged or destroyed by fire can be replaced, albeit with possible disruption to business operation. By contrast the full value of the intangible asset of intellectual property can never be restored once it is lost, either to the customer (who might otherwise have come back for more work which he feels able to do himself if he acquires the company's IPR), or to a competitor (who may well be able to make use of the information without actually infringing the IPR).

Setting aside the daunting prospect of a detailed thesis on IPR, the principal risk lies in possible obligations to hand technical information over to the customer. Although this may be required through the life of the contract, the topic is covered in this chapter for convenience.

The company's best position is one where no rights are granted whatsoever. However, care must be taken as a contract which, for example, includes specified design work but which is entirely silent on IPR may appear to achieve this position for the company. The risk is that the 1988 Copyright, Patents and Designs Act vests ownership of commissioned designs in the commissioner of the work (ie the customer) and not the designer, unless there is an agreement to the contrary. An agreement to the contrary is best recorded in the contract which should therefore ideally include a simple statement that all IPR vests in the company and no rights whatsoever are granted to the customer. This ideal and simple position is not likely to be easy to secure as customers who are paying, for example, for design and development work may want, as a matter of policy, and need, as a matter of practical application, to acquire some rights in the IPR.

In discussing this issue with the customer at the time of contract negotiation, a weather eye should be kept on future business prospects with that customer. A stark unwillingness even to discuss may be enough in itself to make the customer go elsewhere. Alternatively, granting the customer free, unfettered rights in everything is to prejudice the opportunity that might otherwise have existed of the customer having to come back for more. 'Knowledge is power' is nowhere truer than in the minefield of IPR exploitation.

Any grant of rights by the company should be as limited as possible. The first step is to restrict the rights to data which is actually deliverable under the contract and then to limit the definition of what is deliverable. Then, when it is time to deliver the data, the detail put into the deliverable material should be as sparse as possible so as to be minimally compliant with the least onerous interpretation of the definition! 'What they haven't got, they can't use.' In any event, every effort should be made to grant rights only in that IPR generated under the contract. Any pre-existing IPR brought to the contract by the company should be excluded from the grant. Indeed, any and all such 'background' knowledge should be excluded.

If possible, any grant of rights should be in principle only and an express statement should be included in the contract that detailed terms will be agreed later. Apart from the fact that agreements-to-agree are difficult to enforce both legally and in practice, this leaves the door open for future negotiations on the terms (both fees and further restrictions!) at a time when the customer, having become captive, has much less bargaining power than at the pre-contract stage when the full heat of competition is bearing down on the company.

When rights are being granted the extent of the rights should be considered carefully. Supplying software to a customer carries the implied licence that he is free to *use* it. This is obviously sensible since it is absolutely inherent in the intended purpose of the contract. Nevertheless, that use can be limited to a particular place and to particular machines. The right to copy can again be limited. Sticking with the example of software, the right to copy might be expressly limited to the implied right to copy for back-up and security purposes only. In granting the right to modify there can be an implied obligation that the customer must be put into a position where he can actually exercise that right, eg by handing over all the technical information necessary for that purpose regardless of whether that information was expressly deliverable under the contract.

A further restriction is to limit the rights to the customer, only denying him the right to sub licence or assign the benefits or otherwise so as to prevent him from passing the information outside of his organisation and potentially into the hands of competitors.

Whatever the extent of the rights granted, the company should ensure that the recipient of sensitive information or data, (whether just the customer or in the worse situation his subcontractors and other third parties) is bound by obligations of confidentiality. Confidentiality agreements, which are sometimes known as Non-disclosure Agreements, primarily bind the recipient not to disclose the information without written permission, to safeguard it and to use it only for a specified purpose. This last point provides another opportunity to restrict the rights being granted. To enhance the degree of protection the company might consider requiring individual recipients as well as corporate recipients to enter into such agreements. Whether the information is actually disclosed under the terms of the contract subject to conditions of confidentiality, or whether it is disclosed under a full licence agreement, the two overriding aims are to RESTRICT AND PROTECT. Restrict the rights. Protect the information.

In some ways the greatest danger is that, despite the terms of the contract, many personnel working on the contract who may either be ignorant of or not understand the IPR provisions of the contract, may just give the information away anyway in the naive belief that if the customer is paying he must automatically own all the IPR. Allowing this risk to exist is unforgivable and it can be avoided by including a clear briefing on the IPR position at the Contract Launch Meeting (see Chapter 3).

Finally, it should be remembered that in addition to protecting the information by the terms of the contract and any supplementary confidentiality or licence agreements, consideration should be given to statutory forms of protection (eg patents and design registration) and to practical measures such as the use of bold (in both senses of the word) copyright legends on documents and software, procedures to prevent unintentional release and an awareness campaign centered on the abiding first principle of IPR:

'It's ours, they can't have it!'

RISK – BREACH OF THIRD PARTY IPR.

Do
a) Identify all IPR issues at the bid stage.
b) Secure comprehensive licences from subcontractors/suppliers.
c) Grant specific licences to the customer.
d) Secure indemnities from subcontractors/suppliers.
e) Secure indemnities from the customer.
f) Insure against the risk.

Don't
a) Ignore IPR.
b) Give indemnities.

If protecting the company against the risk of its IPR being compromised is a big enough challenge, then equally demanding is dealing with the risk of infringement of third party IPR.

In many projects the IPR situation is a minefield of conflicting interests and requirements (Figure 8.3).

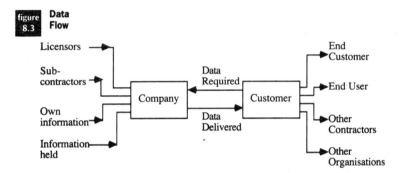

figure 8.3 Data Flow

For these purposes the word 'data' is used very generally to describe any information which may be protected or protectable by an intellectual property right. So this might range from copyright material (eg drawings, specifications, computer software) through design information (eg the unique shape or appearance) to patent details (the essence of an invention) and even the use of trademarks/names (eg product names and logos).

Coming into the company will be data from licensors, subcontractors and perhaps teaming partners, each of whom may be providing data which they own, have licensed from someone else or have stolen (intentionally or in innocent ignorance of a proprietor). The company's own data may be a combination of that which is genuinely the product of its own efforts, that which it happens to possess (ie where the original source is obscure) and that which it possesses as a result of other contracts. Data produced under other contracts may have intellectual property rights vested in the relevant customer(s), the company, third parties or combinations thereof. Data delivered to the customer may be destined for his own use or to third parties under licence or contract, each of whom may have further needs beyond their own use. Each link in the chain may

177

need rights to possess, use, copy, merge or modify the data which it handles. Each may need the right to sub licence, assign, sell or otherwise dispose of the data. Each may wish to secure intellectual property right protection for its part or parts of the whole work. Each may want exclusive rights in jointly created data. All data transmitted may be governed by confidentiality agreements. Data may have come into the possession of individual parties legitimately, by breach of some restrictive agreement by that party, by breach of some restrictive agreement by another party or because the public domain now includes that data.

Thus, if for the purposes of this discussion, the first and second parties are the company and the customer, then all the other parties shown (ie which may have a contractual relationship with customer or company) plus any others remote from or not ostensibly linked to the chain are the third parties from whom lies the risk of allegation of breach of intellectual property right. Any such third party may allege a breach of intellectual property right. On the basis that prevention is better than cure, the lowest risk approach for the company is to ensure that the entire 'IPR picture' is clear and that all necessary licences and permissions are in place in writing. The sooner this is done the better. It is hardly ideal to supply the customer under contract with copies of subcontractor copyright work, only then to find that the company had no right to make such copies. Apart from the unplanned, additional cost of settling with those parties whose intellectual property rights have been innocently or intentionally (?) breached, there is the much higher impact (although probably lower probability) risk of injunction which could bring the whole operation to a standstill. Take a chance on someone else's intellectual property and you 'bet the company'.

Lack of time and impracticability sometimes prevent full researches being done and the proper measures being put in place prior to bidding or prior to making a contractual commitment to the customer. In these circumstances the company is exposed to the risk of alleged breach of intellectual property rights and, following the principles of good commercial risk management, if a risk is carried then opportunities should be sought to pass to someone else the consequences of the risk materialising. The best approach is to seek indemnities from both 'providers' of data (ie licensors, subcontractors etc) and 'consumers' of data (ie the customer). The logic to use with the providers is that they are the experts in the genesis of their products and data and must easily be able to offer an indemnity unless there is something to hide! With the customer the logic is surprisingly similar. Only the consumer can know to whom and for what reason data may be disclosed. Hence he too can surely provide an indemnity unless there is something to hide! Notice that the company appears to know nothing about anything! This position of innocence is a good one but for the fact that in most cases of breach of intellectual property rights, innocence is no defence. Hence the importance of the company being protected by indemnities from both data providers and data consumers that pass to them the responsibility for defending claims and the liability for the cost of defence, the cost of settlement and, in the perfect case, the cost of any consequential effects such as the disruption to the company's operation.

If avoiding the risk is not feasible, if passing the consequences elsewhere is not an option, for example because the providers and consumers do not agree to offer indemnities, then the last option is to insure the risk. Indeed this is a common policy for companies to hold but, nevertheless, this should not be seen as a 'soft' option. 'We needn't worry because it's covered by insurance' is a wholly unacceptable and dangerous ethos.

This essay should be sufficient to show that the greatest risk lies in simply ignoring the problem. Education of all concerned within the company as to the principles of intellectual property rights is in many ways the best form of practical protection. The subject is seen as a black art for obscure experts and while the legal, statutory, procedural and international dimensions of intellectual property matters should not be underestimated for a nano-second, the rules of simple self protection should be understood by all.

Returning momentarily to the issue of indemnities, there is a straightforward rule which says that if it is good to be the beneficiary of an indemnity, it must be bad to be the benefactor. The only possible benefit to the company in giving an indemnity would be to limit the scope and monetary value of a liability which might otherwise be by implication an open-ended liability.

RISK – A THIRD PARTY IS INJURED.

Do

a) Appoint a product safety officer.

b) Ensure that operating manuals are comprehensive on safety.

c) Use hazard warnings.

d) Seek indemnities from suppliers.

e) Insure the risk.

Don't

a) Dispose of records.

Thanks to the privity of contract rule, in most cases only the customer has a contractual remedy against the supplier in respect of defective goods. Goods which do not meet the requirements of the contract or are not fit for purpose may allow the customer various remedies designed to rectify the situation. However, these are not necessarily defective goods. A defective product has the special meaning that it is 'a product, the safety of which is not such as persons are generally entitled to expect'. This introduces the idea that defective products are those which may cause personal injury or death. Thus a corporate customer cannot suffer as such but third parties, such as individuals who work for the customer or who are innocent bystanders, may suffer as a result of defective products. Since these third parties, by definition, are not a party to the contract they must look for a remedy other than a contractual one. The law of tort allows an injured party action against the manufacturer but he must prove negligence which can be extraordinarily difficult. The 1987 Consumer Protection Act overcame this by imposing a so-called strict liability on various entities in the supply chain in respect of injury or death caused by a defective product.

Under the Consumer Protection Act the injured party only has to show that the product was defective, that it led to the injury and that the defendant produced the product or otherwise falls within the ambit of the Act. For these purposes products include goods, electricity and products incorporated in another product, but not immovable things. Injury is death, personal injury and damage to domestic property but the remedy excludes damage or loss of or lack of utility in the defective product and consequential financial loss. Liability for defective products lies with:

a) The producers.

b) Persons who hold themselves out as producers.

c) Persons who, in the course of business, import the product into the EU intending to supply it to another.

d) Suppliers who, after a request by the person injured, fail to identify to him within a reasonable time persons listed in (a) – (c).

Although the Consumer Protection Act is intended primarily to protect consumers, it is clearly the case that a company not trading in consumer transactions can still be liable to injured third parties if, for example, it produces goods for incorporation into products that find their way into the public domain.

With these risks in mind the company should appoint someone who takes responsibility on behalf of the company for ensuring that in all stages of a product's life – design, manufacture, use – the highest regard is paid to safety aspects. The safety of a product is not limited to its intrinsic characteristics. The packaging and operating instructions are equally important and every effort should be made to draw attention to features or applications which pose a hazard.

If the company's products incorporate the products of suppliers then, although the supplier's products may be at fault, the company's liability is not diminished but protection can be sought in the form of an indemnity from the supplier in favour of the company against the financial consequences of a defective product claim against the company.

Defective product or product liability insurance is also a common form of protection carried by many companies.

The risk in defective products is of long life. Action can be brought within three years of the injury or within three years of the injured party becoming aware of the injury, whichever is the later. However, there is an outer limit of ten years from the date on which the defective product was supplied. If a claim is made, the possible defences are:

a) Development risks, meaning that the company must show that at the time the product was marketed the available scientific and technical knowledge meant the defect could not have been discovered at that time.
b) Products 'not supplied' eg if they were stolen.
c) Contributory negligence. The injured party caused or contributed to the injury.

The longevity of the liability and the means of defence indicate the importance of retaining design and manufacturing information and related material for a long time, perhaps even beyond the time at which the product is no longer made or sold at all.